New Brunswick Theological Seminary

To Second Reformed Church,
New Brunswick, church of David D.
Demarest and of many, many
connections with New Brunswick
Theological Seminary
with appreciation
John Coakley
Dec. 17, 2014

The Historical Series of the Reformed Church in America

No. 83

New Brunswick Theological Seminary
An Illustrated History, 1784–2014

John W. Coakley

William B. Eerdmans Publishing Company

Grand Rapids, Michigan / Cambridge, UK

© 2014 Reformed Church Press
All rights reserved

Wm. B. Eerdmans Publishing Co.
2140 Oak Industrial Drive SE, Grand Rapids, Michigan 49503
PO Box 163, Cambridge CB3 9PU UK
www.eerdmans.com

Printed in the United States of America

ISBN: 978-0-8028-7296-8

Library of Congress Cataloging-in-Publication Data

Cataloguing data applied for and in process.

To my students at NBTS,
past and present,
with affection

The Historical Series of the Reformed Church in America

The series was inaugurated in 1968 by the General Synod of the Reformed Church in America acting through the Commission on History to communicate the church's heritage and collective memory and to reflect on our identity and mission, encouraging historical scholarship which informs both church and academy.

www.rca.org/series

General Editor
    Rev. Donald J. Bruggink, PhD, DD
    Western Theological Seminary
    Van Raalte Institute, Hope College

Associate Editor
    George Brown Jr., PhD
    Western Theological Seminary

Copy Editor
    Laurie Baron

Production Editor
    Russell L. Gasero

Commission on History
    James Hart Brumm, MDiv, Blooming Grove, New York
    LeeAnna Keith, PhD, New York, New York
    David M. Tripold, PhD, Monmouth University
    Douglas Van Aartsen, MDiv, Ireton, IA
    Matthew Van Maastricht, MDiv, Milwaukee, Wisconsin
    Linda Walvoord, PhD, University of Cincinnati

Contents

Illustrations — ix
Sponsors — xi
Foreword — xv
Preface — xvii

Part One

    The Reformed Dutch Church and Its Seminary, 1784–1850 — 1
        The "Professorate": Early Years — 1
        The City of New Brunswick — 6
        Getting Organized — 11
        The Superintendents and the Brotherhood of the Ministry — 12
        Reformed and Conservative — 14
        The Office of Ministry and the "Evil" of Student Preaching — 16
        Milledoler and the Superintendents — 17
        The Course of the Covenant — 21

Part Two

    A Face to the World — 27
        The Campus — 27
        A Well-Appointed Institution in Public View — 35
        Gardner Sage's Vision — 38
        Becoming "Eastern" — 40
        African Americans — 43
        World Mission — 44
        The Gospel and Society — 49
        The Seminary and the Synod — 51

Part Three
- Ends and Means, 1920–1973 . . . 55
  - The Plan of 1923 . . . 55
  - President Demarest and the New Era . . . 58
  - The Election of Professor Worcester . . . 62
  - A New Confidence . . . 67
  - New Brunswick and Foreign Missions . . . 70
  - The 1960s: The Shaking of the Foundations . . . 70
  - A "Unified Administration" and a New Approach to Seminary Education . . . 76
  - Postscript: Hiram Street . . . 80

Part Four
- A Commitment and Its Implications, 1973–2014 . . . 83
  - The Vision of Howard Hageman . . . 84
  - An Opening: Evening Education . . . 86
  - Sequels to Diversity . . . 89
  - The Presence of Women . . . 94
  - "The Reformed Church's Seminary," Revisited . . . 96
  - Programs: A Glimpse . . . 100
  - Once Again, A New Campus . . . 103

Endnotes . . . 109
Sources for Images . . . 116
Index . . . 117

Illustrations

John Henry Livingston	1
Livingston's Dissertation	2
Early version of what came to be the "professorial certificate"	3
Garden Street Church	4
Erasmus Hall	4
Charter for Queen's College	4
Ira Condict	5
New Brunswick in 1844	6
Early sketch of Old Queens	7
19th century view of the Old Queens campus	8
John Henry Livingston's house	8
New Brunswick in 1829	9
Livingston in his later years	10
David D. Demarest	12
Philip Milledoler	13
John De Witt	14
Alexander McClelland	15
James Spencer Cannon	16
Title page of Marck's Medulla	18
David Abeel	19
Borneo flora	20
Elihu and Clarissa Doty	21
Amoy, China, mission area	22
John Van Nest Talmage	23
Rutgers College in the late 1850s	25
William Campbell	28
Early view of Hertzog Hall	29
Reading in Hertzog Hall	30
Early winter view of the campus	31
Western end of the seminary campus	31
Map of the completed campus	32
James A. H. Cornell	33
James Suydam	33
Gardner A. Sage	34
Suydam Hall	34
East end of the seminary campus	34
The completed campus	35
Peter Quick	36
Gardner A. Sage Library	38
Talbot Chambers	39
Sydney Noe, assistant to John Van Dyke	40
Original and modern interior views of Sage Library	41
John Charles Van Dyke	41
John De Witt	42
Egbert Winter	43
Islay Walden	43
John Bergen	44
John W. P. Collier	45
Abbe Livingston Warnshuis	45
Jared Scudder	46
Samuel M. Woodbridge and Jacob Chamberlain	47
Horace Grant Underwood	47
Saemoonan Presbyterian Church	47

William V. V. Mabon	48
James Cantine, John Lansing, and Samuel Zwemer	48
The Arabian Mission Hymn	49
Graham Taylor	50
Abraham J. Muste	51
Samuel Merrill Woodbridge, faculty, and students	52
Front entrance to Hertzog Hall ca. 1920s	56
J. Frederic Berg	57
John H. Gillespie	57
William H. S. Demarest	59
Students and faculty in the early 1930s	60
Students and faculty in 1921	61
Map of the campus	62
Sesquicentennial celebration in Sage Library	63
Edward Strong Worcester	63
Milton Hoffman	65
John Walter Beardslee, Jr.	66
Joseph R. Sizoo	67
M. Stephen James	68
Hugh Baillie MacLean	69
Wilbur Washington	70
Walter Marion de Velder	71
Henry Stout	71
Justin Vander Kolk	72
The moving of the Missionary House	72
Demolition of Hertzog Hall	74
Construction of Scudder Hall	74
Zwemer Hall Chapel	74
Completed Scudder Hall	75
Wallace N. Jamison	76
Worship in Zwemer Chapel	77
Paul Fries and students at swearing in ceremony	78
Norman Thomas, Herman Ridder, VIrgil Rogers	79
The campus, ca. 1970	83
Howard G. Hageman	85
Howard Hageman with student Robert Hoffman	85
Paul Fries, Charles Wissink, Hugh Koops, John W. Beardslee III, Virgil Rogers	86
Benjamin Alicea and students	87
Button promoting the Evening Theological Education Program	88
Zwemer Hall at night	88
St. John Hall at St. John's University	89
James Seawood, Richard Sturm, and John W. Beardslee III	90
James Seawood with student Alma Mack	90
Archie Richmond and Jay Do Yu	91
Warren Dennis at his Inauguration	91
Rufus McClendon, Jr. in the Great Hall of Sage Library	92
Korean Student Association (KOSAN) gathering	93
Anti-racism poster mounted in the Hertzog Room	94
Chapel scene in Zwemer Hall, ca. 1975	95
Eileen Winter Esmark, class of 1978	95
Seminary graduates lining up outside Old Queen's	96
Elizabeth Johnson preaching	96
Robert A. White	97
Norman J. Kansfield	98
Gregg A. Mast	98
Poster for the Center's first conference	99
Dean Willard Ashley	100
Some faculty and administration in 1990	101
Certificate in Theological Studies graduation	102
Eilia Tema with Robert White	103
Adjunct, affiliate and regular faculty, 2013	104
Apse of Sage Library before renovation	105
Dedication of Scholte reading court	105
Exterior of new building at night	106
Exterior of new chapel	106
Interior of new chapel	106
Aerial view of New seminary campus with Rutgers campus	107

Sponsors

The following individuals and organizations have helped to underwrite the expense of the publication of this book.

Names as provided by the subscribers

Raphael & Jacqueline Almeida
Rev. Dawn May Alpaugh
Anonymous
Rev. Roberta A. Arden
Richard Arline
David & Lynn Armstrong
Tanya Raggio-Ashley, MD & Willard Ashley, D.Min
Rev. Dr. Charles R. Ausherman
Rev. Paul & Mrs. Ellen Babich, NBTS '52
Violet Barrett Paterson, Ph.D.
Rev. Robert W. Barrowclough
Mary Belasco
Rev. Dr. Gennifer Benjamin Brooks
Mr. & Mrs. Robert C. Berenbroick
Mr. & Mrs. Frederick J. Berenbroick

Rev. Dr. Leonard L. Bethel, NBTS '71
Rev. Donna M. Bevensee
Albert B. Bieber
Tim & Carolyn Boersma
Martha Bonsal Day
Tom & Jane Bos
Donald A. Boulton, M.Div, Ed.D.
Richard L. Brihn, NBTS '69
George & Willa Brown
Dr. Donald J. Bruggink
Kathleen & James Hart Brumm
Rev. Sheila R. Burns-Owens
Rev. Dr. Nathan & Kara Busker
Rev. Lou & Mrs. Joyce Buytendorp
Yasha Carpenter People

Sally Ann Castle
Jaeseung Cha
Rev. Karen M. Chavis
John Chone-Jun Chen
Rev. Dr. Joseph Cho
Marcella A. Christie, M.Div.
Rev. Dr. Tabiri M. Chukunta
Margaret Coakley
Mary Coakley-Fields, Brian Fields & Samuel Fields
Philip Coakley & Julia Kelly
Robert G. Conway, Jr.
Deborah Cordonnier
Tom Culley
Nancy Curtis
Rev. Dr. Charles T. Daniel
Rev. Dr. James Elton Deas, Sr.
Rev. Stacy Deerin
Anna & David Dethmers
Rev. Jack Donohue
Rev. Stephen Eckert
Rev. Eleanor J. Edwards
Mary M. Einhorn, NBTS '06
Christina J. Eldridge
Leah Ennis
Revs. Mark & Pamela Ennis
Rev. Timothy Espar
Minister Barbara Feaster
Barbara A. Felker, MS, M.Div
Adrienne Louise Flipse Hausch, NBTS '95
Martin Eugene Flipse, NBTS '15
Douglas W. Fromm
Peggy Funderburke
David F. Geddes
Walter J. Geldart
Rev. Gary John Gerth, Pastor
Rev. Dr. Doris Glaspy

Rev. Harold J. Goldzung, Sr.
Rev. C. Jeanette Goodson
Rev. Nathaniel T. Grady, Sr.
Rev. Dr. William A. Greene, Jr.
Elizabeth E. Hance
Forrest & Mary Harms
Rev. Kathryn P. & Mr. Peter E. Henry
Arthur B. Hessinger
Dr. John E. Hiemstra
Lucille & Robert Hoeksema
Revs. Craig Jay & Jan Luben Hoffman
Rev. Ihn Ho Huh, Pastor
Martha & Wilbur Ivins
Allan Janssen
Rev. Dr. Lynn & Rev. Dr. Jeff Japinga
Sharon D. Johnson
Franco Juricic
Lewis E. Kain
Dr. & Mrs. Leonard V. Kalkwarf
Norman & Mary Kansfield
Rev. David & Margaret Kasper
Rev. Dr. Myron Jacob Kaufman
James Jinhong Kim
Robert Kokesh
Dr. Norman & Joyce Kolenbrander
Rev. Dr. Cornelis G. Kors
Rev. Dr. Mark A. Kraai
Hartmut & Susan Kramer-Mills
Rev. Dr. LL Kroouze DuBreuil
Rev. Brad Langstraat
Ramona & Robert Larsen
Rev. Bruce G. Laverman
Ran & Jewel Lawson
Rev. Inok Lee
Joyce Yea-Eun Lee
Rev. Roger M. Leonard

Sponsors

Dorothy M. Lewis, ABS, M.Div.
Rev. Cynthia A. Liggon, M.Div. '07
Ronald D. Lokhorst
Joy Lynch
Gregg & Vicki Mast
Peter G. Maurer, NBTS '88
Rev. Nickolas & Linda Miles
Rev. Nicole Simone Mitchell
Dr. Bonard Moise
Rev. Shirley & Ms. Phyllis A. Montanari
Ev. Crystal Moon-Boulware
Rev. Michael J. Moran
Zoë V. Morris
Rev. Dr. Fred Mueller
Najah Munir
J. David Muyskens
NBTS Women's Auxiliary
Milton & Marilee Nieuwsma
Rev. Dr. Joanne J. Noel
Prof. Victor Nuovo
Dr. Richard Otterness
Rev. & Mrs. Adolf A. Pagliarulo
Donald Pangburn, NBTS '59
Rev. Carole A. Paynter
Jeanette Peralta
Rev. Antonio Porter
Loraine Priestley-Smith
Cathy Proctor
Melissa Raak
Rev. Lois Elaine Randolph
Una & Roland Ratmeyer
Rev. Kenneth O. Richardson
Revs. Elmer & Florence Ridley
Carlos Rivera
Chap., Lt. Col., Michael Romano, USAF, Ret.
Eileen L. & Richard E. Rosfjord

Rutgers Canterbury House
Ethel Salamone
Darell J. Schregardus
Alice Scott
Minister Ruth Scott, MA, THM, LAC
Rev. Dawn L. Seaman
Robert Shaw
Rev. Sandra & Mr. Robert Sheppard
Laura Sinclair
Sue Smith
Dr. Terry A. Smith
Rev. Dr. Evans L. Spagner
Rev. M. Ruth Stubbs Jones
Dr. William B. Sutton, III
Dr. Beth L. Tanner
Rev. & Mrs. David Taylor
Daniel & Sherry Teerman
Norman & Nancy Tellier
Rev. Kenneth D. Tenckinck
Rev. John W. Ter Louw
Rev. Megan E. Thomas
Vivian B. Thomas McClain
Cathy Thompson-Fix
Rev. Ann Sutton Van Cleef
Rev. Lynn Carol Van Ek
John Hasbrouck Van Ness
Ronald Vande Bunte
Christopher L. Vande Bunte
Rev. Gerald Vander Hart
James H. & Wanda L. Veld
Gerald L. Vermilyea
Rev. Mr. Frank J. Villerius, BD, M.Div.'66
Rev. Eileen F. Vizcaino, PCUSA, NBTS '08
Robert & JoAnne White
Rev. Bertha E. Williams, M.Div.
Rev. Everett L. Zabriskie, III

Foreword

In 1984, thirty years ago, for our 200th anniversary, Dr. Howard Hageman wrote a history of New Brunswick Theological Seminary entitled, "*Two Centuries Plus*." As the page turns and the seminary moves into a new building and campus and imagines a new future anchored in age old values, Dr. John Coakley offers us another history of the seminary so many of us have grown to love. John has served as our professor of church history since Howard wrote his book, and so in this thirtieth year of his faithful service, he reflects on the evolving mission of this the first theological seminary in North America. The two books don't compete for our loyalty, but rather complement each other.

Through four chapters representing significant eras in our history, Dr. Coakley traces the relationship between the seminary in New Brunswick and the Reformed Church in America. It becomes clear through fascinating stories and remarkable pictures that the seminary and the RCA have both changed dramatically over the years but have never lost each other along the way. With each era the relationship changes, and yet our founding denomination and ecclesial home remains both an anchor and inspiration for our work and witness. And the opposite is true as well, for as the seminary changes it serves as a gentle, and sometimes not so gentle, leaven in the loaf of pastoral ministry.

How has this historic seminary become a national leader in theological education for second career and bivocational candidates? How has the seminary birthed in a dominantly white denomination become such a richly diverse community that is multi-ethnic, multi-denominational and multi-generational? How has this residential seminary for most of its 230 years become a 90 percent "commuter community"? And how have we reassumed our deep and abiding commitment to metro-urban ministry? With each page, you will catch a glimpse of the spirit that has led us on an adventurous and prophetic journey.

New Brunswick Theological Seminary, school of the prophets and deeply committed partner with

God's mission in the world, has taken a new and amazing step in its work and witness. From our earliest days, we have been committed to making theological education more accessible and thus more contextual. Candidates who had for more than a century been sent across the Atlantic to receive their education found a new home at New Brunswick. And with the new home, they received an education that taught them God's mission in a new nation. But we know that we can never rest on the past, for God waits for us.

It was Francis Drake, the world explorer, who wrote a prayer in 1577 which included these words.

Disturb us, Lord, to dare more boldly,
To venture on wilder seas
Where storms will show your mastery;
Where losing sight of land,
We shall find the stars.

This historic seminary has dared to venture on wilder seas, and, in so doing, we have found the stars—indeed, the star of the One who has come to lead us home another way.

Gregg A. Mast, President
New Brunswick Theological Seminary
October 31, 2014

Preface

This volume marks the 230th anniversary of New Brunswick Theological Seminary and the reconfiguring of its campus by retelling the school's history in text and pictures.

The text of the book examines how the *mission* of the school—its fundamental task— has evolved over the course of the seminary's history. As such, though the chapters proceed chronologically, this is not precisely a chronicle. That is, I have not attempted mainly to convey an account of events in chronological sequence, as Howard Hageman did in his admirable history *Two Centuries Plus*, published thirty years ago at the time of the seminary's bicentennial. Instead, in asking about the seminary's mission, I have focused on its changing relationship to the community of faith that it has served, in preparing men and women for ministry.

The narrative proceeds in four parts. The first covers the period from the school's beginning in 1784 through the middle of the nineteenth century, a period when it was so intimately tied to the Reformed Dutch Church as to be inconceivable apart from it. The second part takes the story through the second decade of the twentieth century, showing the seminary's gradual establishment as an institution in its own right, though still uniquely in service to the Reformed Dutch Church, or as it now came to be called, the Reformed Church in America. The third part examines a set of profound changes that occurred in the middle decades of the twentieth century in the relationship between the seminary and the Reformed Church in America, which set the stage for a broadening of the seminary's mission to serve not only that church but also diverse communities of faith that lay beyond it. The final part discusses the subsequent implications of that broadening, over the forty years that have preceded the present moment.

If I have wanted to cast the book as a history of the seminary's mission, I also have experienced another, I hope not incompatible, desire as I was writing it. As a teacher at New Brunswick Seminary for the past thirty years, I have wished that my students had more opportunity to learn about the school's rich history, which they have become a part of, all unawares. And so I hope, for them as well as for all of the seminary's alumni and alumnae, and indeed all its friends new and old, that the book might offer a sense of connection to the seminary's story, and of their own part in its mission.

It is to that end of fostering connections that I offer readers not just the text but also the pictures, especially the photographs, for these photographs have a power all their own to draw us into the seminary's story. They do this through the human faces that engage our eyes across the years and also through the glimpses we get of a certain place in New Jersey that, precisely in its variation of guise over time, we recognize with satisfaction as our own.

I am glad to have this chance to thank several people for their help. First and foremost is Russell Gasero, archivist of the Reformed Church in America, my friend and colleague, who literally made the book possible, through his help locating archival resources, his production design, his management of the images, and his expertise on all aspects of the publication process. I also particularly thank President Gregg Mast, who encouraged and greatly aided the project from the beginning; Cathy Proctor, director of development at New Brunswick, whose enthusiasm for the project helped keep it on track; and Margaret Coakley, for wide-ranging assistance. I am grateful also to the following for invaluable help of various kinds: Matthew Gasero, Ramona Larsen, Laurie Baron, Rett Zabriskie, Bob Belvin, Jackie Oshman, Jinhong Kim, Tom Frusciano, Erika Gorder, Chris Brennan, Willem Mineur, Bethany O'Shea, Lynn Berg, Willard Ashley, Robert White, Norman Kansfield, David Waanders, Paul Fries, Jaeseung Cha, Lynn Japinga, Maria Gasero, Don Bruggink, and James Brumm. And many thanks to the subscribers whose names appear in the pages at the front of the volume, for their cheerful support of its publication.

I add a final word of thanks, to a person in the seminary's history whom I have not mentioned in the text of this book, but on whom I have constantly leaned: Edward Tanjore Corwin (1834–1914) of the class of 1856, scholar, pastor, adjunct faculty member, and sometime rector of Hertzog Hall, whose labors set the example and laid the foundation for any subsequent study of the seminary.

PART ONE

The Reformed Dutch Church and Its Seminary, 1784–1850

The institution that was to become New Brunswick Theological Seminary had its beginning in 1784. That was the year when the American denomination known then as the Reformed Protestant Dutch Church (and since 1867 as the Reformed Church in America) elected one of its ministers, John Henry Livingston, "Professor," to prepare students for the ordained ministry. In this sense the Reformed Dutch Church *created* the seminary. But this did not mean that in its early years the seminary was ever entirely distinct from the church itself, or that "church" and "seminary" could even be conceived apart from each other. Rather, the seminary was embedded in the church's very structure, and, more than that, it was something essential to the church, an almost reflexive expression of the church's life and mission. This was the seminary's sole identity in the early decades.

The "Professorate": Early Years

The election of the professor was a major event for the Reformed Dutch Church, for a very particular reason. For a century and a half—long after the British had taken over New Netherland and made it New York and almost to the end of British colonial rule—the Dutch church in America had remained subordinate to its

1 John Henry Livingston (1746-1825). Portrait by Gilbert Stuart, 1795.

mother church in the Netherlands. The American Dutch, that is, did not have their own "classis," which in the Dutch system is the supervisory body with the authority to ordain ministers. In the Netherlands it had been a firm requirement that candidates for ordination undergo a thorough formation in the Dutch church's doctrine and system of government. To provide this, each classis relied on the services of Reformed professors in the Dutch universities, to whom they had a natural connection within the structure of the established Christian commonwealth of the Netherlands. But that structure had no counterpart in America, so the American candidates for ministry had to cross the Atlantic to be educated and ordained. At least, that was the official policy.

Eventually the church in the Netherlands did acknowledge the need of the Dutch churches in America to be self-determining if they were to survive, and in 1768 gave a tentative blessing for the Americans to create their own supervisory bodies. It did this, though, with the understanding that the Americans would appoint their own professors to prepare candidates for ministry.[1] Consequently, the first constitution of the new American church (its "Articles of Union"), adopted in 1772, made provision for what was called the "professorate," that is, the office of professor, accountable directly to the church's General Synod.[2] The synod was acting on that provision when in 1784 (after a delay during the Revolutionary War years) it elected Livingston, who had received his doctorate at the University of Utrecht in the Netherlands and came recommended by the faculty there.

By placing the education of theological students so directly under central ecclesiastical control, the Dutch Americans' invention of a "professorate" signaled something new in comparison with other Protestant churches in America and even in comparison with its mother church in the Netherlands. Among the English-speaking denominations in colonial America—mainly the Congregationalists, the Presbyterians and Anglicans—the usual practice was for students to prepare for ministry through private study under the informal guidance of a pastor following their undergraduate work; only afterward were they examined by a church judicatory, which had had

2 Livingston's Dissertation

[3] Livingston's template for the "professorial certificate," in which he refers to the candidate as entrusted to him "to be imbued with the arts that befit the minds of theologians... ."

no supervision over their process of preparation. The church in the Netherlands offered some precedent for considering theological professors in the universities to hold the ecclesiastical office of teacher (*doctor*), which, in principle at least (though in practice this was less clear), brought the instruction of theological students under the direct authority of the church.[3] The Dutch Americans clearly had this model in mind. But—in large part because they could not rely upon universities as the mother church did—they gave the office of "teacher" a narrower and more careful definition and structure of accountability than it had in the Netherlands. They understood this ecclesiastical office of teacher to be vested precisely in their "professor," who was answerable to the synod and had as his task the preparation of students for their ecclesiastical examinations. By virtue of his office, he would provide each student a certificate of readiness as a necessary ticket of entry to that examination. Through him, then, the synod directly supervised the preparation of ministers.

The election of Professor Livingston in 1784, however, did not yet put the newly formed "professorate" on a firm foundation, for the synod had designated no funds to support him. Nor was there agreement as to *where* he would do his work. These matters continued unresolved for twenty-three years. Livingston remained a pastor in the Collegiate Dutch Church in New York City during that time, probably teaching his students at home (first at 79 Broadway and later in a house in the Bowery) and without pay except for a "suitable honorarium" of "about five pounds" (as directed by the synod) from each student at the end of his studies. Meanwhile, the synod also authorized another minister, Hermannus Meyer of Totowa, New Jersey (d. 1791), to assist in the instruction, although apparently without giving him the title of professor. For a brief period between 1795 and 1798, the consistory of the New York congregation reduced Livingston's pastoral duties in Manhattan to allow him to relocate across the East River to the village of Flatbush, where he probably met his students in the edifice of the "flourishing academy" of Erasmus Hall, with the understanding that the synod would finally begin to provide

5   *Erasmus Hall, in Flatbush, Brooklyn*

the professorate a permanent home, elected two more professors with the same authority as Livingston: Solomon Froeligh, pastor at Hackensack, and Dirk Romeyn, pastor at Schenectady. Students could choose among the three. This remained the state of affairs for several years. In 1804 the synod recommitted itself to vesting the professorate in a single professor and reaffirmed Livingston in that position, continuing to recognize the other two "during their natural lives" but declaring that they would not be replaced. However, adequate funds were still lacking, and it was still unclear where the professorate was to be settled.[4]

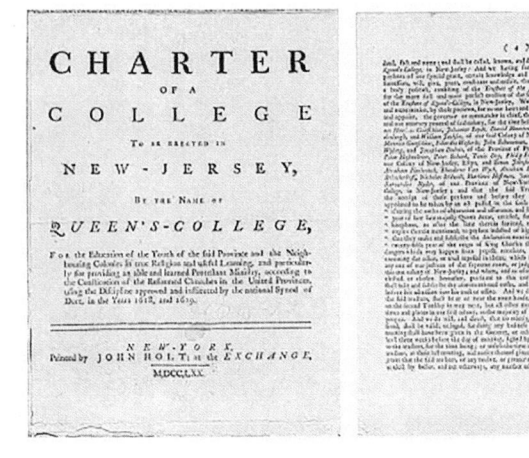

4   *Garden St. Church (built 1693), where Livingston gave his inaugural lecture*

financial support and the professorate could be officially situated there, in effect creating the conditions of a school. But the synod did not follow through on the plan, and in early 1798 Livingston returned to his full pastoral charge in Manhattan. Meanwhile in 1797 the synod, still divided over where—and perhaps even whether—to give

6   *Charter for Queen's College*

The decisive move toward settling the professorate came finally in 1807 when the Particular Synod of New York and the trustees of Queen's College (the future Rutgers College) in New Brunswick, New Jersey, made an overture to the General Synod. Queen's itself had been founded as a Dutch Reformed college, and the framers of its royal charter in 1771 had envisioned it not only as a place of study of "learned languages and other branches of useful knowledge"—an undergraduate school, in effect—but also as a place where "young men of suitable abilities may be instructed in divinity, preparing them for the ministry,"[5] and proposals to locate the professorate there had already been made more than once. The college, strapped for funds, had ceased operation in 1794, but in 1807 its trustees resolved to "revive" it and approached the General Synod in September for its endorsement and help in raising money for that purpose, "especially from the members of the Reformed Dutch Church, for whose benefit chiefly this institution was originally designed."[6]

The synod, seeing an opportunity to resolve the question of the location of the professorate, welcomed the trustees' request, and together—a key figure being the Reverend Ira Condict, minister of the First Reformed Church in New Brunswick who was also a trustee and sometime faculty member of the college—the trustees and the synod devised the so-called "Covenant." It became the basis for the permanent location of the professorate at New Brunswick, as well as the basis of its relation to the college for almost six decades. The Covenant stated the terms on which the synod agreed to cooperate with the trustees in raising money for Queen's, and these were terms that made clear the church's particular interest in the professorate and the synod's resolve to maintain the professorate under its own authority. Thus the Covenant stipulated that all the money raised in the churches of New York (where

7   Ira Condict (1764-1811)

other undergraduate colleges were being established), as distinct from the churches of New Jersey, would be "exclusively appropriated" for the "establishment of a theological School," that is, for the settling of the theological professorate rather than for other purposes of the college; that though the trustees would hold all of the funds designated for the professorate, including any funds raised in prior years, they agreed to "call no professor of theology but such as shall be nominated and chosen by the General Synod" and "bound" themselves to do so as soon as enough money was available; and that there be a "permanent Board appointed by the Synod to superintend the theological institution."[7] Thus the professorate was to be located within, and a genuine part of, Queen's College—the "theological institution" of Queen's—yet it

8 New Brunswick in 1844, showing the railroad bridge and, between the smoke plumes, Old Queen's

was still very much the creature of, and closely controlled by, the synod.

The appeal for funds met with enough success by the summer of 1808 for the trustees to issue their call to Livingston to become professor of theology at Queen's College—and also to become its president, on the understanding that his duties in that office would be mostly ceremonial. After negotiations, he accepted in the spring of 1810. Resigning his pastorate in New York, Livingston moved to New Brunswick on October 10 of that year and took up his work there with his theological students, who were at that point five in number.[8] He was sixty-four at the time and continued in his duties for the remaining fifteen years of his life, a venerated elder statesman of the church.

The City of New Brunswick

New Brunswick in 1810, when Livingston arrived, was a city of perhaps three thousand people.[9] Its location on the main road from New York to Philadelphia and on the Raritan River at the head of navigation made it important as a hub for transportation and markets.[10] That importance was to increase in the 1830s with the coming of the railroad and the Delaware and Raritan Canal and continue with its growth in the latter part of the century as an industrial center.

The trustees of Queen's College, of which the "theological institution" was now part, had laid the cornerstone of the college's new building on a lot in Somerset Street in April 1809. Designed by John McComb,

9 Early sketch of Old Queen's

Jr., of New York (who was also the architect of the New York City Hall), this building is still standing and is known as "Old Queen's." The college moved into the still unfinished structure from its former location at the east end of what is now Monument Square in 1811; construction was finally completed in 1825, the year that "Queen's" was renamed "Rutgers." The building was to be the shared home of the "theological institution" and the "literary [i.e., undergraduate] institution" of the college until 1856. The central portion of the building accommodated classrooms, library, and chapel for both institutions of the college, as well as for the affiliated preparatory school; the two wings of the building served as residences for theological professors.[11] Livingston himself lived

10 Later (ca. 1900) view of Old Queen's (center)

in his own residences—first, at his arrival, at 59 Albany Street, and very soon afterward in a house on the corner of Townsend Street and the street then called Trenton Turnpike, which later in the century would be renamed Livingston Avenue in his honor. But almost all of his colleagues and successors in the theological faculty would occupy the wings of the college building until 1867, when the seminary would build housing for them on its own new campus.[12]

Students, for their part—the theological students as well as the undergraduates—lived in boarding houses in the city in these first several decades of the nineteenth century. The boarding houses must have been a conspicuous feature of the life and economy of the city. We get a sense of their ubiquity in a memoir by David Demarest of the seminary class of 1840 (and faculty member from 1865 to 1898), who remembered that, in his student days in the 1830s, first as an undergraduate and then as a theological student, he lived in a succession of boarding establishments that anyone familiar with the city today can still roughly envision: first "in the house occupied by

11 1922 photograph of John Henry Livingston's house (no longer standing) on Livingston Avenue at Townsend St.

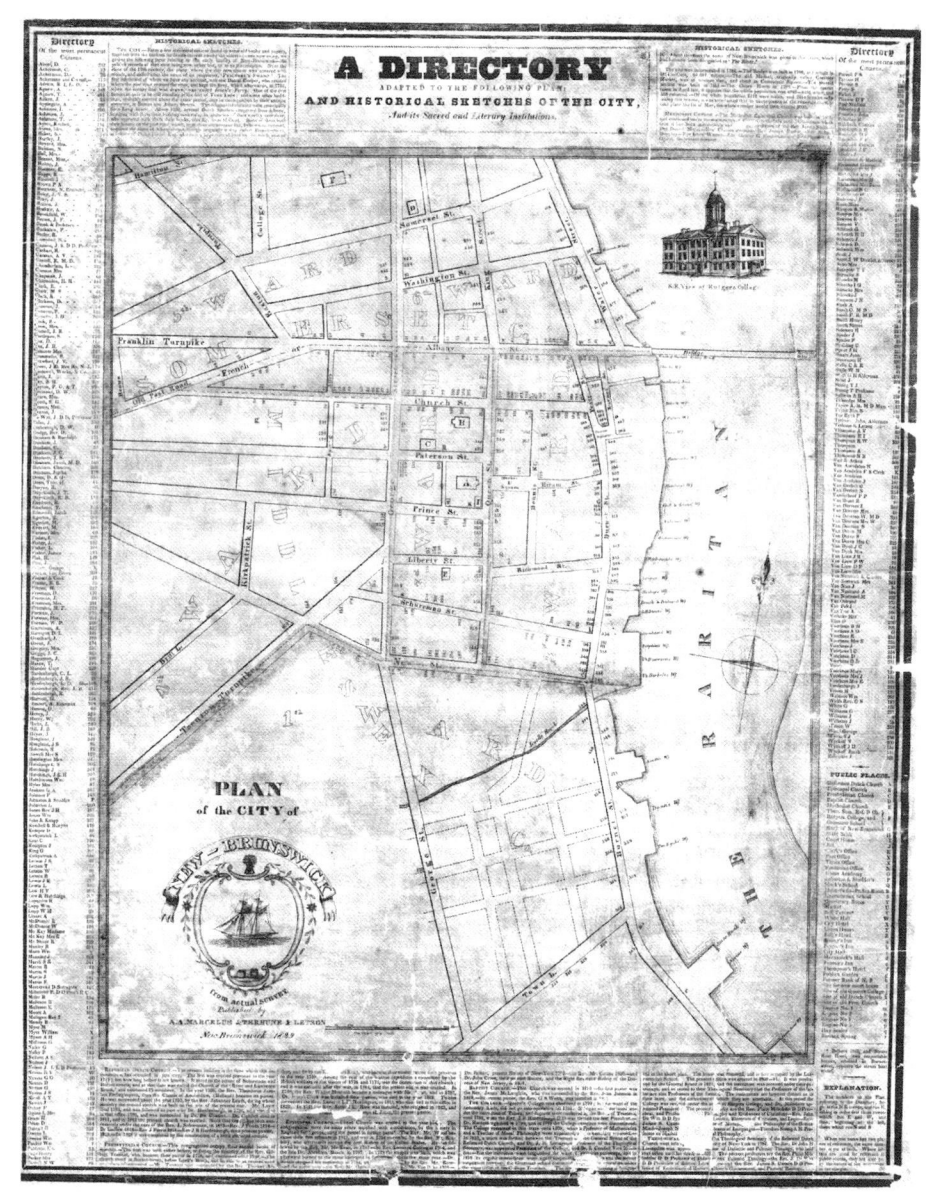

The Reformed Dutch Church and Its Seminary, 1784-1850

12 New Brunswick in 1829. The letter "F" at the top of the map marks the place of Old Queen's.

13 Livingston in his later years

Dr. Ball, corner of George and Church Streets," later "at a Mr. Sutphen's on the north side of Albany Street, corner of Spring Alley [Spring Street]," then at "William Letson's in Albany Street," then "with Mr. Freedman in Somerset Street...."[13] Prices for these establishments were, however, unstable,[14] and the superintendents worried periodically that the rising cost of board beyond their ability to influence it would cause students to go elsewhere—a concern that was no small factor in the superintendents' eventual decision to establish their own campus with a dormitory system in 1856.[15]

Such was the city where the seminary was settled and took shape. But before we turn to the story of the school's forming, it is important to note one more element in the environment, namely the slavery of African Americans, a ubiquitous presence even when not immediately visible in our sources. We know that Livingston—who, by any evidence that has come to light so far, did not pronounce publicly on the subject of slavery—had grown up in Poughkeepsie, New York, in a family that owned slaves and had almost certainly owned slaves himself as late as 1790 while he was still in New York City, although by 1800 he apparently no longer did so.[16] Moreover, Livingston's father-in-law (and cousin), the prominent New York merchant and signer of the Declaration of Independence Philip Livingston, from whom he and his wife inherited some, at least, of their wealth, had likely had a financial interest in slave ships owned by his father, i.e., Mrs. Livingston's grandfather.[17] The college's—and thus the seminary's—connections with slavery also included a more diffuse and less easily pinpointed sort, because slavery remained very much a part of the economy and the fabric of society in the city of New Brunswick as in New Jersey and New York generally, even long after "gradual emancipation laws" were passed in those states in 1799 and 1804 respectively,[18] and the seminary, like all institutions in the society, did not avoid being implicated in it. For instance, David Demarest remembered that in his childhood in the 1820s in the Dutch culture area of northern New Jersey, "most all the thrifty farmers in Bergen County owned one or more slaves"[19]—and these Dutch laymen would have come from the segment of society that had earlier responded to the subscription for funds for the college after the Covenant of 1807, and that would continue to respond to such appeals. At any rate, the fact of the interweaving of the seminary's early history with the history of slavery is beyond doubt and, as the antiracism initiative within the seminary in recent years (of which, more below) has urged, our open acknowledgment of it is called for, as well as further research into the points of contact and discussion of their implications for the seminary today.

Getting Organized

In 1812, after Livingston had been in New Brunswick for two years and the new college building had opened its doors, the General Synod adopted a thousand-word document called "Plan for a Theological School," which was to be the constitutional basis of the seminary at New Brunswick and determine its structure of authority. It establishes the General Synod as the school's "paramount authority," enumerates the powers of the Board of Superintendents, describes the duties of professors and students, and specifies the three-year "course of study" which is to cover "natural, didactic, polemic, and practical theology; biblical criticism; chronology and ecclesiastical history; the form and administration of church government; and pastoral duties" and the "original languages" of scripture, with a final examination at the end and punctuated by two vacations each year. [20]

This plan for the seminary at New Brunswick was roughly contemporaneous with the published constitutional plans of the two new institutions that were to be the most influential American seminaries of the first half of the nineteenth century, namely the nearby Princeton Seminary (1811), and Andover Seminary in Massachusetts (1808). But the New Brunswick document is much shorter than either of the other two, and New Brunswick Seminary's difference from those other institutions—a difference that reflects its origin—can be seen in what its plan omits.

The founding of Andover and that of Princeton were major events in their own right; a major motivation for each was to ensure the orthodox Calvinism of the professional ministry in the churches they served, over against the multifaceted perceived threats to that orthodoxy in American culture, in the colleges, and in the churches themselves. Accordingly, each of those plans includes an extensive prologue declaring the institution's purposes. And in details, the concern for orthodoxy shines clearly. Thus the Andover plan specifies that each professor, upon election, subscribe publicly to the Westminster Catechism, as well as to another creedal statement that was apparently particular to the institution, and declare that he will maintain the faith against "Atheists and Infidels" as well as "Jews, Mahometans, Arians, Pelagians, Antinomians, Arminians, Socinians, Unitarians, and Universalists" and "all other heresies and errors ancient or modern which may be opposed to the gospel of Christ or hazardous to the souls of men"; and he must repeat this declaration to the trustees every five years.[21] The plan of Princeton charges its board of directors to "inspect the fidelity of the professors," as well as their morality, competency, and faithfulness to Presbyterian principles, all on behalf of the General Assembly, granting them specific disciplinary powers. It also specifies that each professor will not only subscribe to the "Confession of Faith, Catechisms, and Form of Government of the Presbyterian Church" at the time of his inauguration, but will also "lay before the board of directors... a detailed exhibition of the system and method which he proposes to pursue," and "make such alterations or additions as the board shall direct" so that the curriculum corresponds precisely to the direction of the board.[22]

By contrast, the New Brunswick plan—though it follows the Princeton plan closely as regards the structure of governance and the content of the curriculum—omits any statement of purpose and makes no allusion to the dangers of infidelity, except to say obliquely that "the Board [of Superintendents] shall be competent to... inspect the doctrines taught by professors, and the general course of study...." It is not that the Reformed Dutch Church was unconcerned to uphold orthodoxy; on the contrary, faithfulness to the Reformed standards of belief had been a concern behind the establishment of the professorate years before, and the Constitution of the Reformed Protestant Dutch Church already provided for professors to promise publicly that they would teach in accordance with those standards, and it clearly explained their amenability to the General Synod.[23] But that is just the point: unlike Andover or Princeton, New Brunswick Seminary did not come into being in response to the faith crises of the first years of the nineteenth century. It had no new purpose; it was indeed not a new institution but an elaboration of an existing one, which had come into being some twenty-eight years earlier in the rather different circumstances of the Reformed Dutch Church's assertion of its status as a self-determining American body, indeed as a guarantee of that status. The *esse* of the institution did not have to do so much with defense of orthodoxy *per se*—though orthodoxy was certainly expected—but rather with the condition *behind* its amenability, namely its organic connection to the Reformed Dutch Church.

The Superintendents and the Brotherhood of the Ministry

The superintendents embodied the close connection between the seminary and the church. From the beginning, their role exceeded what we would think of today as governance and came very close to a role of

14 David D. Demarest (1819-98), class of 1840, faculty 1865-1898

administration—a hands-on role, that is, in which they assumed many duties and tasks that today would fall to the faculty in most institutions. Indeed, unlike the faculty at Princeton, who had collective powers to discipline and even dismiss students at their discretion,[24] the New Brunswick faculty was not constituted originally as a body to take collective action, and even when it began to be such a body,[25] the superintendents still had the final word on all cases of discipline and dismissal.[26] As specified by the plan, the superintendents, at their annual meeting at the end of the academic year, collectively oversaw the final oral examinations of every course under every professor—a practice that, with some variations in procedure, lasted well into the twentieth century. Apparently in the very early years the superintendents felt free to professors present in an "advisory" capacity.[28] And from 1824, at the direction of the General Synod, all new students were "admitted exclusively by the Board of Superintendents," through a special annual meeting for that purpose at which they interviewed candidates[29]—again a practice that continued into the twentieth century.

Another sign of the intimate connection of the superintendents to the life of the seminary was that new faculty members tended to be nominated from their ranks. In these early decades the chosen candidate was in almost every case someone who was both a prominent pastor at the time of his election and also was either a present or past member of the Board of Superintendents.

Thus Philip Milledoler, who was one of the ministers of the New York City (Collegiate) Reformed Church when he was elected as Livingston's successor in the chair of didactic and polemic theology on the latter's death in 1825, had also been by that moment a member of the Board of Superintendents for a decade, and Milledoler's own successor, Samuel Van Vranken, elected in 1841 after having served a series of Reformed congregations, had also been briefly a member of the Board of Superintendents two years earlier.

John Schureman, who was called in 1815 to occupy the new second professorial chair, that of ecclesiastical history and polity, had been a charter member of the Board of Superintendents in 1812, when he was pastor of the Reformed Church in New Brunswick. Upon Schureman's death in 1818, John Ludlow, who had been Schureman's successor as pastor of the New Brunswick church after being a star pupil at the seminary, succeeded him on the faculty, and though Ludlow had not then served as a superintendent, he was to do so later during his long tenure as pastor of the Reformed Church in Albany, before rejoining the faculty later in his life, in 1852. Ludlow's successors after his departure for Albany were

15 *Philip Milledoler (1765-1852), faculty 1825-1841*

interpose their own questions among those of the professors, though in 1830 they officially resolved to delay their questions at any given examination until the professor signaled that he had finished.[27] The superintendents also in these years received detailed reports from the professors about the content of their teaching and did not simply approve revisions in the curriculum but actually determined them. In 1825, at the faculty's request, the superintendents formed a committee to "revise the whole plan of studies of the theological college," with the

16 John De Witt, Sr. (1788-1831), faculty 1825-1831

both superintendents at the time of their elections: in 1825 Selah Woodhull, who was at the time a pastor in Brooklyn, and then after Woodhull's death less than a year later James Spencer Cannon, who was minister of the Six Mile Run church not far from New Brunswick, and who indeed had been a member of the Board of Superintendents.

John De Witt, minister of the Second Reformed Church in Albany, likewise was a member of the superintendents when he was elected to the third professorial chair, that of biblical literature, when it was established in 1823. Alexander McClelland, who succeeded De Witt in 1832 and was at the time of election a member of the faculty of Rutgers College, was the one professor in this period who had neither served as a trustee nor come directly from the parish ministry, although he had earlier served as a Presbyterian pastor in New York City.

Faculty members, therefore, had typically seen the seminary from the vantage point of the superintendents, as agents of the General Synod; moreover—what is perhaps their deeper connection—they came directly from the ministry of the local church and thus from the brotherhood of ministers. The seminary itself was in fact an active expression of that brotherhood and is perhaps best understood, in this period, as an extension of it—a place of familial nurture and discipline of its prospective members. To that end, the hands-on character of the superintendents' involvement in the school and the timidity with which the faculty emerged as a collective body with its own authority in this period are not surprising. Though the seminary was spoken of as an "institution" in its own right—indeed had been so from the pre-New Brunswick days of the professorate—still it was an institution separated from the church whose creature it was only by very porous boundaries. To put the matter slightly differently: the church—or more precisely, the church's ministry—did not delegate *to* the seminary the task of preparing ministers, as though it were an agency apart, however faithful; instead, the church tended to think of the seminary as a function of its own agency and thus to operate it directly.

Reformed and Conservative

Although in this period New Brunswick Seminary faculty members did not have wide reputations beyond the bounds of the seminary and the Reformed Dutch Church, they reflected the theological currents of the time, as the Reformed Dutch Church encountered these.

Probably the major theological debate of the time that affected the seminary was around the question of the role of human "means" in effecting conversion, a question made pressing by the revivalism that touched all evangelical churches. The Reformed Dutch, keen for signs pointing to spiritual awakening in its churches, as shown by the synod's yearly "State of Religion" reports, was also, like the so-called Old School Presbyterians of the time, resolutely orthodox in its resistance to any perceived suggestion that regeneration involved human agency. So, in 1834 the synod called Professor Alexander McClelland to explain a sermon he had published that appeared to contain just such a suggestion when he said, for example, that the impenitent sinner "may procure the *grace* of regeneration," just as a hungry person may find food "by an easy process of plowing, sowing and reaping."[30] Though the synod was satisfied with McClelland's explanation, in which he asserted his belief that seemingly human "means" are themselves actually "the instruments by which God executes his sovereign purposes," it censured the sermon nonetheless.[31]

Such a concern to avoid the suggestion of a human role in regeneration also constituted a theme of the one major monograph published by a New Brunswick faculty person in this period, James Spencer Cannon's *Lectures on Pastoral Theology*. There Cannon— wary perhaps of the "anxious bench" and the other "new measures" of, for instance, the New-School Presbyterian Charles Grandison Finney— showed himself very cautious about revivals, saying that occasionally, but only occasionally, the Holy Spirit may regenerate many people in the same place at the same time and that often what seem to be revivals are not revivals at all but occasions for the collective expression of human irrational sympathy, fear, conformism, or self-righteousness.[32]

17 Alexander McClelland (1794-1854), faculty 1832-1851

Revivalism also entered, though from a different direction, into another controversy that touched the Reformed Dutch Church in this period and had echoes in the seminary. This was the controversy over the so-called Mercersburg theology, that is, the teachings of John Williamson Nevin and Philip Schaff at the German Reformed seminary in Mercersburg, Pennsylvania. Nevin's and Schaff's conception of Christian faith as a historical entity that had developed organically involved a critique of revivals as shallow and individualistic in the light of such a view of the church (a critique different, we note,

1852, Joseph Frederick Berg, who had been Schaff's and Nevin's chief opponent within their own denomination, left to join the Reformed Dutch Church, and, in 1861, the General Synod elected Berg professor of didactic and polemic theology at New Brunswick, where he served until his death in 1871—thus in effect enshrining at New Brunswick the opposition to Mercersburg. [33]

The Office of Ministry and the "Evil" of Student Preaching

A curious theme appears again and again in the minutes, one that suggests something about the meaning that the church attached to the seminary that we might not otherwise guess at, since it exhibits a concern rarely heard nowadays, if at all. This was the strong aversion to allowing students to preach in the churches until they completed their seminary work. Apparently consistories and pastors persisted in inviting them to their pulpits, and students persisted in accepting—but this was a state of affairs that exasperated both faculty and superintendents in the extreme. The superintendents repeatedly issued prohibitions, beginning in 1818 and with the repeated endorsement of the General Synod, but to little avail. The rules were briefly relaxed in 1851 to allow seniors to preach in specific churches at specific times under the supervision of the professors, because preaching to "promiscuous audiences" is indeed "highly important as a preparation for future duties"—thus some experience in preaching might be a good thing for students—but this logic did not prevail, and the decision was rescinded the next year by the synod itself. Then, in 1858, the synod required the superintendents at the time of the annual examinations to "inquire" personally of every student whether he had "conformed" to the resolution against student preaching. In 1860, outraged that

18 James Spencer Cannon (1776-1852), class of 1796, faculty 1826-1852

from Cannon's), and also a critique of the cherished Protestant conception of the Reformation as a clean break from a corrupt Catholic Church, and by implication of the fervent anti-Catholicism of American Protestants. A shocked reaction to Mercersburg among the Reformed Dutch in the mid-1840s effectively ended what had been a strong movement toward intentional cooperation between themselves and the German Reformed. Then in eleven students had answered "no" to the annual inquiry the previous year and that the number had gone up to twenty-one in the present year, the synod went further, empowering the faculty and superintendents to suspend any student who answered "no" to the inquiry, "until his case can be reviewed by the next General Synod."[34] After this, there were no more negative answers recorded. In 1872 the annual inquiry ceased, but the policy continued in effect.[35]

Why was it so important that students not preach? Clearly, occasional comments to the contrary, it was not simply a matter of keeping students intent on their academic work, for the faculty and the superintendents often lauded students' work in Sabbath schools and in the New Brunswick community (such as pastoral work with sailors at the docks), all of which certainly took them from their studies. The point was that the students' completion of their work as students is precisely the requirement for entry into the office of minister of the Word, of which preaching is the signal function. It is the fulfillment of an elaborate set of requirements for that entry; it calls attention to and reinforces the boundary that sets that office apart to protect its authority. In this sense the students have a kind of liminal status that was a stage in the process of attaining to the office of ministry, and for that very reason they had to be defined clearly in distinction from it. To, in effect, enter the territory of the office before one has met the requirements is a violation of the whole order of things, an undermining of the system. As a committee of the synod declared in 1860, "If the members of the Seminary be 'preachers,' they are no longer 'students.' And if they be 'students,' they are not 'preachers.'... And, in point of fact, we believe it to be undeniable, that even three years, to say nothing of one year, do not produce any more valuable and ripened fruits, than the necessities of ordinary intellects and the interests of sound doctrine require. Your committee believes that this unlicensed license, and the constitution of our Theological courses of training for the pulpit and the pastorship, are absolutely incompatible; and that, for order, for discipline, for law, for truth, one must overcome the other."[36]

Milledoler and the Superintendents

In 1841, Philip Milledoler, who sixteen years earlier had succeeded Livingston as professor of didactic and polemic theology, resigned his position in the aftermath of a student petition complaining of his teaching. For a professor to leave the seminary under a cloud was a very unusual event, but the way the matter was handled stands as a demonstration of the church's sense of intimate ownership of the seminary. This attitude was not unusual at all, but was in fact the great determining force in the seminary's early history.

The incident unfolded over a few months' time. The students petitioned the superintendents in February, objecting to what they perceived as the professor's rote use of the textbook, which was the "Medulla" (*The Marrow of Christian Theology*) of the seventeenth-century Dutch theologian Johannes à Marck. They found the Latin difficult, the workload overbearing, and the classroom style stultifying. The superintendents, having received the petition, heard Milledoler out on the issue at a specially called meeting in May. He made some comments about the students that the superintendents understood as counter-charges, but when he refused to put these in writing—saying that he had only intended to ensure that the superintendents considered the students' complaints in context—the superintendents considered the comments withdrawn and declined to take account of them.[37] When they then referred the matter to the synod, which met in June, the focus was squarely on the substance of the students' complaint—on Milledoler's pedagogy, in other words. The synod appointed a special committee, which reported that instruction at the seminary needed to "call forth, to a greater degree, the exercise of the powers of the mind, as well as secure an increased amount of knowledge of the important doctrines of the gospel." It also appointed another committee that convened in New Brunswick in July and formulated a detailed plan calling for the textbook to serve only as a "guide" for Milledoler's teaching, specifying the succession of subfields that he should follow over the students' three years and directing him to provide them with recommendations for their reading, direction, and a "full, copious system of questions" from which their year-end examinations would be drawn. Milledoler protested several points of the plan as onerous and unworkable and declared that it "has the appearance of being framed for the express purpose of coercing the Professor to retire"[38]—and when the synod at a special meeting in September adopted the plan with only minor changes, he submitted his resignation, registering his "entire dissatisfaction with all the proceedings which have led to this result, from the reception of the memorial to the present hour."[39]

The superintendents and the trustees seem not to have hesitated to act as they did. From the evidence we have, Milledoler's own conclusion that he was being forced out doesn't seem far-fetched. But even the professor himself said that he did not question "the abstract right" of the synod to "prescribe to their Professor the course of instruction."[40] And in the end the synod prescribed it in considerable detail, without—as far as the sources allow us to see—any ambivalence about its own competence and authority to do so. It was the church's seminary.

JOHANNIS MARCKII

CHRISTIANÆ THEOLOGIÆ

Medulla

DIDACTICO-ELENCTICA,.

EX MAJORI OPERE, SECUNDUM EJUS CAPITA, ET PARAGRAPHOS, EXPRESSA.

In usus primos Academicæ Juventutis.

EDITIO PRIMA AMERICANA,

ACCURATE EMENDATA, ET POST EXPRESSOS SCRIPTURÆ TEXTUS

INDICE DUPLICI,

GUILIELMO AB IRHOVEN AUCTORE,

TUM RERUM, TUM LOCORUM S. SCRIPTURÆ, QUÆ OBJECTIONUM MATERIAM VULGO FACIUNT, EXPLICATORUM AUCTA.

PHILADELPHIÆ:

TYPIS ET IMPENSIS J. ANDERSON,
13, N. Seventh Street.
1824.

19 Title page of Marck's Medulla

The Missionary Enterprise

Mission, understood as the spreading of the gospel both in the expanding United States and in foreign parts, was a central concern of all American evangelical churches in the nineteenth century. The Reformed Dutch Church was no exception, and it saw the seminary as key to its own contribution to mission. As the superintendents declared to the General Synod in 1839,

> ...when we remember...how many openings in providence of a most favourable character for the enlargement of our church are presented; and how loud and how affecting the calls from the distant and perishing heathen, for the messengers of Christ to break to them the bread of life; *we are urged to renewed diligence and prayer for the prosperity of this seminary of sound science.*"[41]

The students had a missionary organization that embodied these concerns. This group originated at an early moment, probably in 1811, and no doubt under the influence of Livingston, who was then already a well-known advocate for the missionary cause. Known at first as the "Berean Society," in 1820 it renamed itself the "Society of Inquiry on Missions."[42] A continuous run of the society's minute books has survived in the seminary archives, extending from 1839 well into the twentieth century. The minutes are refreshingly candid at points, reminding us that these young men, apprentices for the brotherhood of ministers, were indeed a group of adolescent males who jostled each other for dominance or influence, gave and received insults, defended their honor, or left the room in a huff. They were clearly absorbing skills and expertise for the leadership roles that would eventually be theirs. They engaged (especially early on) in debates on the fundamental issues; in March 1839, for example, the question was, "Is it by teaching letters and civilization to the young or by preaching that heathen lands will sooner be evangelized?"[43] Or they read essays to each other on missionary topics and (especially as the church's own development of foreign mission

20 *David Abeel (1804-1846), class of 1826*

fields progressed in the forties) resolved collectively that new missionaries would arise from their society. They also carried on a wide correspondence with missionaries both at home and abroad, and with mission societies, including the student societies at other seminaries. Typically one student would be designated to draft a letter, which would be later read aloud and "ordered to be sent," sometimes with revisions. They also presented "intelligence" reports to each other about the missionaries and their work, gleaned from publications or personal contacts.[44]

Although the seminary's heyday as a school for missionaries was still to come (see below), it produced several notable figures for foreign fields already in these first few decades in New Brunswick.

The earliest and probably best known of these missionaries was David Abeel (1804–1846), who grew up in the city of New Brunswick, came under the influence of Livingston through the First Reformed Church where his family attended, and then attended the seminary, graduating in 1826. After a brief pastorate in Athens, New York (1826–28), and though always in ill health, Abeel spent the rest of his life traveling, including two extended sojourns in East Asia as an agent of the American Board of Commissioners for Foreign Missions, assessing mission prospects and promoting the missionary cause through his writings.

Then between 1836 and 1842, with Abeel's encouragement, no fewer than nine young New Brunswick graduates, along with six spouses and one unmarried woman, became the first persons from the seminary to settle abroad as long-term missionaries. Their field was the remote island of Borneo; they became the "Borneo Mission," and their story is a poignant one. Several worked with the Chinese community that had settled on Borneo; others worked with Malays, still others with the indigenous Dayak people. They were determined and optimistic about their work, but there were many obstacles, including language, the hostility of Muslims, and extreme difficulties of travel within the island. Abeel himself wrote after visiting that he had never seen "a field so barren, so uninviting." When, after the First Opium War in 1842, China had to open its doors to foreign missionaries, at Abeel's urging those of the Borneo missionaries who had learned Chinese—at that point Elihu and Clarissa Doty and John and Theodosia Pohlman—were transferred there as charter members of what would become a thriving mission in southern China, at Amoy. That same year, after the return of one missionary to America for reasons

21 Frederick B. Thomson (1809-1848), class of 1834, one of the Borneo missionaries, gave these watercolors of plants of "the East" to the Society of Inquiry

22 Elihu Doty (1810-1864), class of 1836, and Clarissa Doty (1806-1845), misionaries to Borneo and China

of health and the death of another, the work with the Malays came to an end. It was the work with the Dayaks that held on, with the missionaries determined to continue even though, as they wrote in 1846, "to the present time no visible success attends our labors," and indeed at the end of the mission's history there would be no conversions to point to. That end came in 1849, when the one remaining missionary, William H. Steele, returned to America. For years, Steele continued to promote the mission, hoping to resuscitate it. As late as 1852, the General Synod was saying "that as a Church we will not yet abandon Borneo; but with earnest prayer to God for his blessing, will carefully and anxiously seek to reoccupy that station."[45] This was not to be. But the determination and spirit of the missionaries—not to mention what strikes us now as a kind of austere innocence—still shine through the sources and reflect the earnest piety that the seminary had cultivated.

Another missionary graduate of special note from the early decades was John Van Nest Talmage of the class of 1845. A year after graduating, he presented himself for service in China with the Amoy Mission, sailed there in 1847, and remained a member of the mission until 1889. Talmage distinguished himself as an evangelist and translator but is perhaps best remembered for leading the mission's resistance to the General Synod's resolution in 1863—never implemented—that the mission should form a classis of the Reformed Dutch Church. In arguing against this action, he was the first among the Reformed Dutch Church's missionaries to state and defend the now fundamental principle of world mission, that missionary churches abroad should, as E.T. Corwin put, "not be mere continuations of the denomination whose missionaries had founded them, but should have an independent existence their own."[46]

The Course of the Covenant

The covenant between the Reformed synod and the trustees of Queen's College continued in effect for sixty years after its adoption in 1807. It underwent revisions, however, as conditions changed. The church's principal interest in the college was as a school to prepare students for the seminary—to provide the first stage, that is, of the education of ministers. But as the college strengthened, the church's support became less necessary and the church's expenditure of resources on the college's behalf indefensible in the minds of many ministers and elders—after all, the interests of the sem-

23 Amoy, China, mission area

inary had always been the church's priority—so that by mid-century, though the covenant was still in place, it was losing its reason for being.

In the early years the college was in dire need. It had been the trustees of Queen's who had taken the initiative to propose the original 1807 covenant at a moment when the college had been closed for some years, as a means to revive it. Though it resumed full operation soon after the covenant was agreed upon, it remained understaffed and underfunded, and for almost two decades it was not the undergraduate work but "the theological work," that, as W.H.S. Demarest later wrote, "was strong and uninterrupted, the dominant element in the [Queen's] institution's life."[47] As funding of the seminary proceeded apace, with support for the second theological professor in place by 1815, and for the third by 1825, funding for the college languished. Recognizing this, in 1814 the synod adopted a plan, put forth by Livingston, to make Queen's itself into a "theological college" that, while still an undergraduate institution, would be largely staffed by the theological professors, would adopt a more specific focus on the preparation of candidates for admission to the seminary, and would afford only limited space for students intending other careers. But this plan failed for lack of funding, and the undergraduate college closed down again in the fall of 1816. It would remain closed for nine years. The trustees, moreover, were at that time deep in debt from construction costs. After having incurred the synod's displeasure by paying some of the debt out of the fund designated for the theological professorate, in desperation the trustees offered in 1822 to sell the college property to the synod outright. The synod was initially very reluctant. It feared to be bound, pointing out, in the words of the Board of the Corporation, that it was not in fact committed to "always have a Theological College at New-Brunswick."[48] Eventually, however, in 1824, it did agree to the sale for an amount that exactly covered the trustees' debts and took over responsibility for the property, making some needed repairs that same year. Meanwhile the college remained closed.

In 1825, the college reopened one more time and, as before, it did so on the basis of the covenant with the synod. For though the college had hardly prospered in the years since 1807, the covenant had in fact given Queen's a continuous existence even when there were no undergraduates. When the trustees, encouraged by a promise of subvention by the Collegiate Church of New York, proposed the reopening, they framed it as a re-establishment of the proper scope of the institution

24 John Van Nest Talmage (1819-1892), class of 1845, missionary to China

overall, putting "both its Theological and Literary departments, in complete operation," as the covenant had envisioned. They also reminded the synod that the "the speedy revival of the Literary exercises in Queen's College is highly important to the prosperity of the Theological Seminary...."[49]

But if this new revival of the college built upon the old covenant, it also moved a step beyond it: the trustees and the synod agreed upon a new version of the covenant, which did not merely keep the institution open as the 1807 version had done but aimed more specifically at making the undergraduate college viable—with important implications for the seminary. For now the theological professors would have it as part of their jobs—on the basis of the salaries paid them by the synod—to serve the college directly, and in very specific ways. One of them would be obliged to serve as president of the whole institution, including the college (which indeed had been the case with Livingston, but only as a matter of a separate salary agreement with the trustees), and all of them were to "have such literary duties assigned them in Queen's College, by the General Synod, as the synod shall deem best calculated to promote the mutual interest of both institutions"—in other words, they were to work with undergraduates as well as with seminary students. They were, in fact, to be responsible for much of the college's curriculum in the humanities—specifically "belles lettres" (literature) and the various branches of philosophy—in addition to taking responsibility, on Sundays, for undergraduate students' "Biblical recitations" and for a weekly homiletical "discourse."[50]

The Covenant of 1825 did indeed mark the beginning of the permanent resurgence of Rutgers College. But the church was never quite reconciled to it. In W.H.S. Demarest's words, "The real practical question at bottom chiefly was the wisdom and fairness to the seminary of the very considerable service given by the theological professors to the college classes."[51] In 1832 the synod appointed a committee to investigate whether the covenant was "in its present form beneficial to the grand object proposed by the endowment of said Seminary, and to confer on the necessity of a change; and if it be necessary, on the practicability and form of its modification, or the expediency of its entire abolition."[52] The committee could not agree on a report to the next synod and was discharged, but the covenant had clearly become a sore spot; in 1836 another synod committee blamed the paucity of seminary students at that moment on, in part, the negative impression conveyed by the professors' "*double engagements... in two institutions*" and the consequent diffusion of their energies.[53] Professor McClelland, meanwhile, repeatedly denied that he was obliged to teach in the college, a denial which in turn issued its own complaints that McClelland's stance violated the covenant.[54]

Eventually, in light of the dissatisfaction within the church, the covenant was revised twice again in quick succession in 1839 and 1840, but the idea of the covenant was now unmistakably beginning to lose its appeal. The 1839 version considerably reduced the theological professors' duties in the college, declared that "no theological professor shall hereafter be the president," and committed the synod to finding funds for a president who would devote full time to the position.[55] Then, in 1840, the synod's attempts to raise the money having been "met by discouragements," the covenant was revised yet again, to call for the trustees to find the funds to pay the college's president, and for the "whole administration" of the college to be entirely in the hands of the trustees, and to declare that the synod "repeals, on its part, all former action on this subject, which may or can interfere with the tenor of this resolution." We hear now, as a stated rationale for all of this, that the college has its own "form and machinery" for governing itself, and the synod's involvement amounts to interference.[56]

For several more years, the college reported to the synod, and the seminary professors continued to offer some instruction in the college, and scholarship funds for college students continued to receive attention from the synod. But in essentials the trustees were now on

25 *Scene of Rutgers College in the late 1850s by T. Sandford Doolittle (1836-1893), class of 1862, who was later a long-time Rutgers faculty member. The new Hertzog Hall of the seminary (see Part II) is just visible in the distance behind the Rutgers' president's house on the right.*

their own. A committee of the synod in 1850 concluded that "the connection effected between the Synod and the Trustees by that covenant is for all practical purposes virtually dissolved," even though various legal connections, including the synod's ownership of the college property, and the sharing of that property, required that the covenant continue as a legal arrangement, which was to be the case until 1867. Taking all of this into consideration, there was no reason why the trustees and the synod could not begin to cultivate "a more harmonious relationship."[57]

αϖ

The demise of the covenant in the years around 1850 conveniently marks, in retrospect, the end of the seminary's formative years. The seminary would never afterward entirely cease to be what it had been in those early decades: an organic part of the Reformed Dutch Church, based in the office of professor and thus in the very structure of the church, and an extension of what I have been calling the church's "brotherhood" of ministers. But it would soon have a location of its own apart from the college, and there in that new place it would start, at least, to have—while never apart from the church—a certain new life of its own as well.

PART TWO

A Face to the World, 1850–1920

From the middle of the nineteenth century through the first two decades of the twentieth century, New Brunswick Theological Seminary was still very much an organ of the Reformed Dutch Church (from 1867 called the Reformed Church in America,[RCA]), a seedbed for its leadership, and a focus of its affection and pride. But something new entered the self-awareness of the leaders of the institution and the way the church viewed it. Its position changed subtly as the RCA incorporated new Dutch immigrants who arrived during the period and who themselves instituted a school for ministers in 1866; from that moment, New Brunswick was no longer *the* seminary, but rather *a* seminary, of the church. At the same time, the seminary had more direct encounters with worlds beyond the Reformed Church—especially with academic culture, the broader religious culture of evangelical America and, increasingly, the emerging urban industrial American society. In this sense it began, at least, to acquire an identity of its own.

The Campus

In 1856 the seminary finally moved its classes out of Old Queen's into a building exclusive to itself, and over the next three decades it would build a full-fledged campus apart from that of Rutgers College. This new campus was to be a point of pride for the Reformed Church and a sign of confidence and optimism about the seminary's place not just within but also beyond the church.

The decision to leave Old Queen's took shape in the superintendents' meeting of 1854, as a response to two pressing concerns. One of these was the old matter of student housing. Students told the superintendents that it cost them "three and four dollars a week" in the boarding houses, with a prospect of a fifty-cent increase the following fall, whereas at Union Seminary in New York, which provided lodging in its own buildings, the cost was only $1.96, and at Princeton Seminary it was even less; moreover, students endured "suffering and sickness" out of efforts to "live within their means" and

1   William H. Campbell (1808-1890), faculty 1861-1863

even so were accumulating debt. "At least five" had gone to other seminaries, where it was cheaper to live.

The other concern was crowding in the college. Again, the immediate impetus was a complaint from students, who had been put up to it, in part anyway, by a faculty member, the blunt William Campbell, professor of biblical literature. He had told them in his classroom one day (as W.H.S. Demarest would later tell the story from the oral tradition) not to "stand" having to share space with the college any longer, but to "have a meeting, make protest," to "get the synod or the Collegiate Church or someone to build a theological hall for the sole use of the seminary." At the meeting of 1854 the superintendents, proud and confident about their institution, agreed that the time was ripe. "There is hardly another denomination equal to us in means, in this land, that is without such a building. We ought to have it. We must have it. If the people of the church be told of the situation of our seminary we will have it. And that in a twelvemonth." They appointed a committee to make plans and resolved to bring them before the General Synod, which approved it the following year.[1]

Once put into motion, the plan for a new building was realized swiftly. Within a year, local landowners, chief among them the merchant James Neilson, had donated land that formed a tract between College Avenue and what soon afterward became the extension of George Street, and Anna Hertzog of Philadelphia had given $30,000 to fund the building itself, to be named "The Peter Hertzog Theological Hall," after her deceased husband. The cornerstone was laid November 8, 1855. The building was dedicated September 23, 1856. At the superintendents' meeting that May, they had registered their pride at the sight of the rising structure and their anticipation of a bright future for the seminary.

Already the "Peter Hertzog Hall" greets our eyes. Its foundation has been laid, as we believe, with much prayer, faith, and remarkable benevolence, and will be finished during the present season. This will be an important event in the history of Theological Seminary, and of the Reformed Dutch Church. While, then, we contemplate the history of the past, and the

A Face to the World, 1850–1920

2   The early view Hertzog Hall, on the left evokes something of the "desolateness" of its surroundings at first. Even after the rest of the buildings in the campus row were constructed, as in the view on the right, ca. 1900, the Rutgers campus across Seminary Place remained undeveloped.

prospects of the future, and are ready to inquire, "Watchman, what of the night?" with gratitude and reason we can say, "The morning cometh."[2]

The opening of Hertzog itself was only the beginning. The extent of the steady improvements made over the next decade remind us that the campus really was begun from scratch. The summer after the opening of Hertzog, the committee entrusted with the construction reported to the synod that the building "stands in the midst of desolateness," but it promised that "the work of arranging and adorning will be vigorously prosecuted." The same report describes the heating system and the rules of the hall, which gave the faculty oversight, limited residence to students "preparing for the Gospel Ministry," and specified a daily schedule including prayers and set study hours.[3] At the synod of 1859 it was reported that the brickwork had been painted, a fence fifteen hundred feet in length had been installed, and an "avenue in front of the Hall" has been "opened and graded," and trees have been "set out" and a drain "six hundred feet long, and reaching down below the foundation of the Hall has been dug and properly secured, to lead off from the building the water which was settling under it, and rendering it damp and unhealthy."[4] In 1861, the faculty report speaks of physical improvements: a "paved terrace and flight of stone steps leading up from the gate to the front door, the planting of trees, and the paving of College Ave." As for the "sward of the Seminary ground," it was "not yet what it must be. The Faculty find the red shale of Middlesex rather intractable, but purpose to per-

3 Garrett W. Conover, class of 1895, in his room in Hertzog Hall, May 1, 1894

severe in their efforts and expect to conquer."[5] Then in 1864, a "reading room" was outfitted in Hertzog, "supplied with the most valuable periodicals, American and Foreign."[6]

In 1866 an expansion of the campus began, as ground was broken for three faculty residences. Until then the college property still belonged to the synod, and the seminary faculty was still living in the wings of Old Queen's. In 1864, William Campbell, having left the seminary faculty to become president of Rutgers College, had asked the synod to transfer ownership of the college land to the trustees of the college, and the synod did so for twelve thousand dollars, a sum that would constitute a "fund for the purpose of erecting, upon the grounds of the Hertzog Theological Hall, residences for the Theological Professors."[7] Additional money was also raised, and by 1868 three houses had been built—one to the east of Hertzog and two to the west. They began to define the campus as a row of buildings along an east-west axis. Their description in the General Synod minutes of 1867 suggests the continuing pride that the church felt about the great project of the campus as it took shape, as well as the awareness that these buildings would create a public image.

> The houses are of brick, double and of two stories, of sufficient size, as the Synod directed, to accommodate large families. They are very solidly and permanently built, of the best materials, and by the most competent mechanics, under the special superintendence of your Committee and of an experienced architect. They are only sufficiently removed from perfect plainness of finish to save your Committee and the Synod from permanent discredit, as having disfigured a valuable property for the sake of a very small saving of expense. They are now universally approved as creditable to your Committee and to the denomination whose respectability they represent."

The same synod recognized formally that the Covenant was no longer in effect.[8]

There was one more phase in the development of the campus, which significantly advanced that project and brought it essentially to completion. In 1869 it was reported to the synod that expensive repairs and other improvements on Hertzog Hall were needed; that already deterioration of the grounds needed to be attended to, as well some work on the new houses, as "is usual in new buildings, after a year or two of shrinkage and settling, moreover a "fourth house is needed"; and that some of the money that had been pledged for the houses had not come through. In other words, funds

A Face to the World, 1850–1920

4   The seminary row appears behind the unidentified family, at moment was between 1872 and 1884, when the last faculty residence would be built in the gap to the right side of Suydam Hall.

5   West side of the seminary row, ca. 1900

needed to be raised. Therefore, James A.H. Cornell, an 1841 graduate of the school and sometime secretary of the Reformed Church Board of Education, was engaged as an agent "in obtaining the necessary amounts." Over

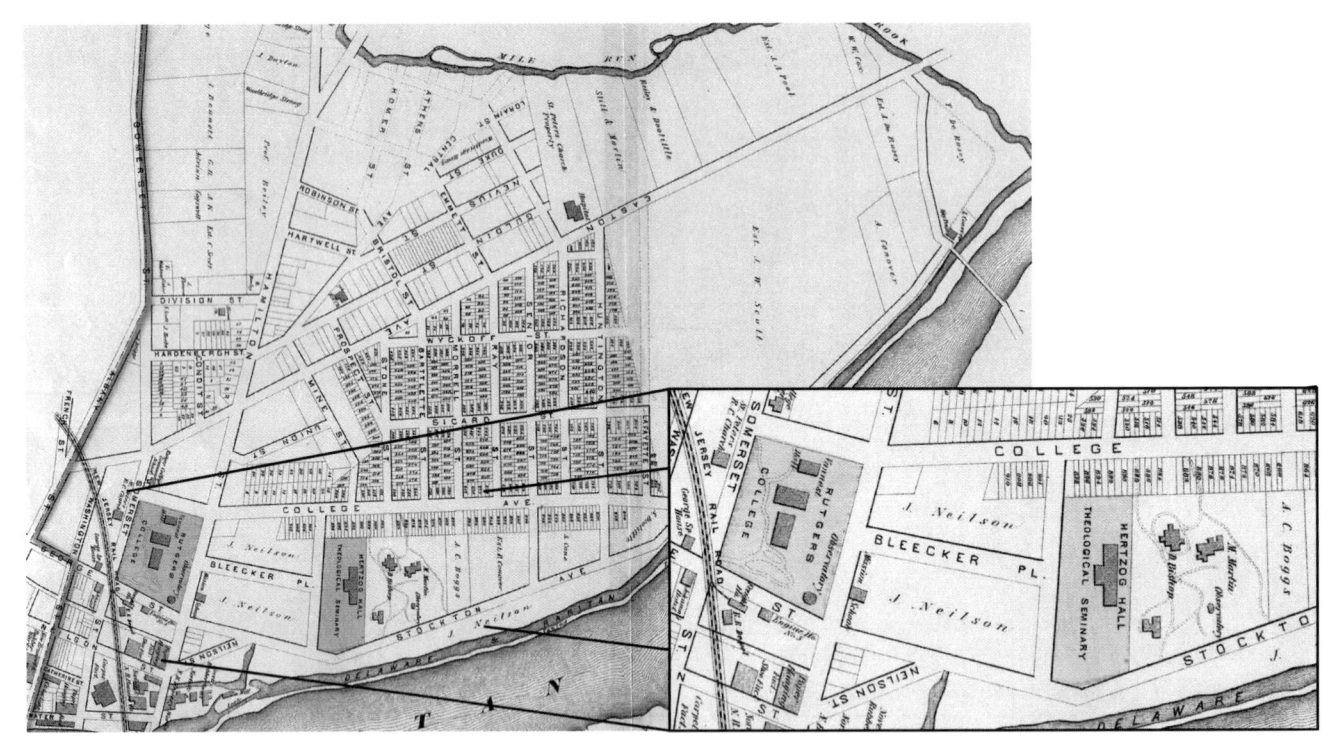

6 This 1876 map shows the seminary campus in relation to Rutgers and to its ward of the city. The campus row would have been almost complete, though only Hertzog Hall is shown.

the next four years Cornell was phenomenally successful; as E.T. Corwin was to write, in that brief period Cornell "completely revolutionized the financial condition of the seminary, by adding considerably more than half a million to its resources, in endowments, buildings and books."[9]

Among Cornell's successes as a fundraiser, his greatest single achievement was to cultivate the interest of two wealthy laymen from New York City: James Suydam and Gardner Sage. Both of these men went on to give liberally both for the endowment of professorial chairs (see below) and also for buildings and their maintenance. Indeed, almost by themselves Suydam and Sage moved the seminary into a new era, in terms of infrastructure and institutional capability. In 1869 Suydam and Sage together financed the purchase (from Prof. Cook of Rutgers) of what was then called the "Stone House" on the corner of George St. and Seminary Place. It was to be occupied by Professor Berg, who had been in rented quarters since leaving the college property—establishing all the professors on the campus. Then Suydam entirely funded the building known as "Suydam Hall," placed just to the east of Hertzog Hall and containing classrooms, a gymnasium, a chapel, and a room for the Society of Inquiry—a multipurpose building that functioned in part, as Howard Hageman has written, as what we would now call a "student center." Sage, for his part, funded a

A Face to the World, 1850–1920

7   James A.H. Cornell (1818-1899), class of 1841

8   James Suydam (1798-1872)

library building, namely the "Gardner A. Sage Library," to be placed on the west side of Hertzog in symmetry with Suydam Hall, the library's cornerstone being laid on the very day that Suydam Hall was dedicated, June 5, 1873. Suydam died in 1872 and Sage in 1883. Both of them made liberal provisions in their wills for the upkeep of the buildings of the seminary, including especially the ones that bore their names. Suydam's will also provided funding for the erection of a fifth professorial residence, which was built to the east of Suydam Hall and completed in December of 1883.[10]

Construction of the fifth professorial house brought the campus to completion. In 1885, in the volume containing the addresses given at the great centennial celebration of the year before, there appears an engraving of the whole ensemble of buildings as they would have appeared from an elevated point southeast of George Street.[11] The image includes the new fifth faculty house (the second building from the right, in recent years popularly known as "Kooy House" after the family of Vernon Kooy, a professor who lived there for a time in the mid-twentieth century). At any rate it celebrates the culmination of thirty years' effort, in the grand idyllic

10 Suydam Hall

prospect of a handsome row of structures that, at that moment, would have rivaled the structures of the college, which indeed it faced squarely across the still mostly empty tract of land that would later be developed as the college's Neilson Campus.

9   Gardner A. Sage (1813-1882)

11 East side of the seminary row, ca. 1900

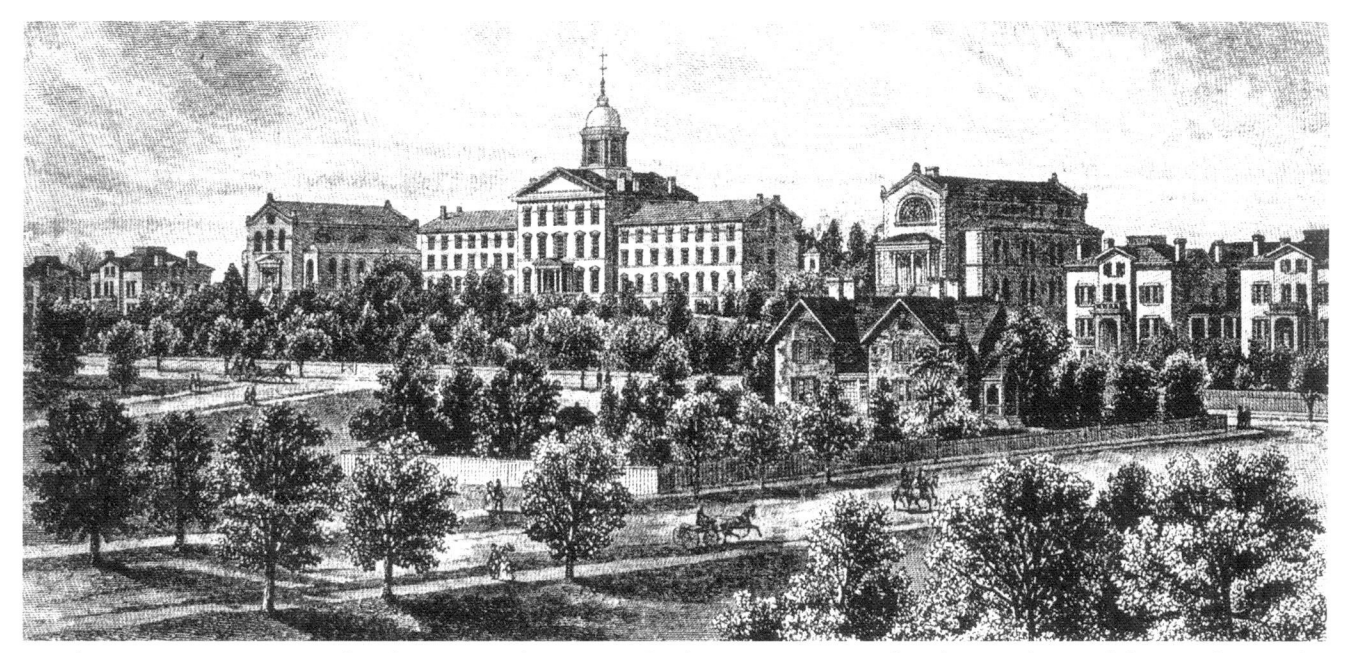

12 The campus, as it appeared in the seminary's Centennial volume in 1885, just after the completion of the grand row. The engraving however predated that completion; the whole harmonious prospect had been long envisioned. See note 11.

A Well-Appointed Institution in Public View

The years when the campus was taking shape also saw increased concern for efficiency and excellence, measured not just in terms of the seminary's utility to the Reformed Church in America but also in terms of a standard set by other institutions, particularly other seminaries. New Brunswick Seminary was indeed set on a hill, with an implied awareness of the public gaze.

An important impetus to this developing self-consciousness of the school was the realization by the superintendents and the General Synod in the late 1860s, in the course of the economic difficulties of the post-Civil War years, that a new approach to funding was needed. In 1868 the superintendents observed that "a comparatively small sum from each of our Reformed Churches would place the Seminary on a level with the most favored Theological schools in this country, so far as concerns the matter of Endowment...."[12] The General Synod later that same year, observing the need for a more "efficient executive management of the local interests of the Seminary," began to envision changes in the composition of the Board of Superintendents (eventually put into place in 1872) to, among other things, include more lay members who had "financial ability."[13]

At the same time the seminary took its first steps toward establishing a focused administrative structure beyond what the Board of Superintendents alone could provide, however competent its individual members. That same synod of 1868 reorganized and elevated the "Standing Committee on Hertzog Hall," which had had a desultory existence until then, to become the executive committee of the Board of Superintendents, to provide oversight of the school's operations.[14]

In 1870 the reorganized Standing Committee on Hertzog Hall (which would be renamed in 1877 the Standing Committee on Seminary Grounds and Property) began printing annual reports, which display the immediate effects of its efforts. In that year, James Suydam chaired the committee, Gardner A. Sage became secretary, David Demarest represented the faculty, and James Cornell was appointed financial secretary "for the collection of funds for the endowment and support of the Seminary, and for the general advocacy of its interests, as prescribed by the Synod"—an illustrious group. The committee reports an inventory of the property and the measures taken to paint Hertzog Hall and repair its heating, plumbing, and drainage systems as well as its roof. The committee also notes the need for renovations to the hall's chapel. It has much to say about the library, then still housed in Hertzog Hall. It was being "remodeled… by the erection of alcoves and cases," and a committee had been formed to "purchase books." We also hear for the first time of a separate library building, though the plan at this point is to place it on the east side of Hertzog, where instead Suydam Hall will be erected.

Then the committee proceeds to report on the subject of the "internal management of the Hall": it has appointed a "Rector," the Reverend Peter Quick, "whose duties shall be the general supervision of the Theological Hall and grounds, the boarding of students, care of rooms, collection of funds from students for room rent, gas bills, &c., and the enforcement of the regulations adopted for the government of the Hall." The committee also reports that Mr. and Mrs. Quick have effected "a complete revolution…in the domestic regime of the insti-

13 Peter Quick (1806-1886), class of 1836, Rector of Hertzog Hall (1869-1874) and Librarian of Sage Library (1874-1886)

tution." Rules are now "observed"; there is "cleanliness, order and domestic comforts."

> When sickness comes, the invalid receives the attention of a Christian family. A plentiful table furnishes excellent fare to all students who choose to avail themselves of it at the mere cost of provisions and servant hire, and without regard to pecuniary profit.

The committee stresses again that "such a system of personal and official superintendence is essential to the welfare of the institution physically, morally and religiously" and that the overall point has been to "make the Hall, not a boarding house, not a refectory, not a commons, but a real and proper Christian Home."[15]

That first report of the Standing Committee is a remarkable document. The idea that the committee intended to oversee the seminary efficiently, like a business, comes across clearly. But it expresses something more as well: an optimistic, even visionary spirit of reform. It is a vision of reform that does not touch only on the physical plant but also on the moral and spiritual lives of the students and the quality of the library. The committee's aim is a large-scale refashioning of the school as an exemplary institution.

An event the next year, 1871, illustrates this spirit of high aspirations. The General Synod elected William G.T. Shedd to the chair of didactic and polemic theology, to replace the recently deceased Joseph Berg. Shedd, a Presbyterian, was at that moment on the faculty of Union Seminary in New York and a widely published theologian of national stature, and his election stood as a radical departure from the church's normal practice of (as we have seen) choosing professors from the ranks of its own ministers in pastoral office. It is not incidental that the committee the synod designated to "wait upon" Shedd to inform him of his election included both Suydam and Sage; their notion of a seminary with reputation and influence well beyond the Reformed Church in America stands in the background here. Shedd eventually declined the position, and the synod elected Abraham Van Zandt, minister of the Reformed church in Montgomery, New York. Thus the synod returned to its old pattern, although Van Zandt had been a parishioner of Suydam some years earlier at the Central Reformed Church in New York City, and Suydam appears to have promised openly to complete the funding (which he himself had begun earlier) of the endowment for the chair if Van Zandt would be elected.[16]

In the 1870s and the several decades to follow, the minutes of the synod and those of the superintendents allude frequently to norms established by other seminaries and to their sense of New Brunswick's standing among those seminaries. A synod committee in 1871, in declaring the need for at least one new faculty chair (the "fifth" chair, to be realized eventually in 1884), envisioned that thereby "the whole scheme of instruction should aim at the broadest and most thorough theological culture, so as to make its advantages equal to the best institutions of the land." And when the synod voted on the reorganization of the Board of Superintendents that year, it put "the powers of nomination in the local Synods instead of the classes, whose choice has too often been accommodated to the personal wishes of their members"—a change the wisdom of which is apparent from "the experience of other theological institutions."[17]

In 1885, the superintendents pointed to the excellence of the facilities at the seminary and their importance for the world beyond the seminary itself, even in the context of a lament over a low student count (which had for long been a periodic feature of the minutes). "Surely something ought to be attempted to increase the number of students, *and thus extend to our own denomination and the entire Church of Christ*, the splendid opportunities here afforded for educating the world's future ministers."[18]

Or again, in 1888 the Standing Committee reported that the "appointments" of Hertzog Hall are "well-nigh perfect, leaving it doubtful if any similar institution in the land affords to the rector and students so many conveniences and comforts."[19] The superintendents also

14 Gardner A. Sage Library

commended the faculty on the growing place of "archaeological and linguistic studies" in the curriculum (owing especially to the work of John G. Lansing, on whom see below) and the roster of visiting lecturers, all of which is evidence that the seminary is "keeping in the forefront of Theological institutions, and constantly increasing its scope and efficiency."[20]

In the superintendents' minutes for 1904, when we hear the first argument for a *sixth* professorship to be established, it is because this will be "necessary if we are to hold our ancient position in the front rank of theological education."[21] Whether or not others would have judged New Brunswick to be in the "front rank" of seminaries at that point, when (as will be seen) its financial support was seriously lagging is another question. But clearly such status was still important to the seminary's self-image.

Gardner Sage's Vision

Awareness of the seminary's public context on the part of its leaders and continual self-comparison with other seminaries became standard fare from this period onward. The high aspirations that characterized the era of Suydam and Sage—to be in the very front rank of American seminaries—would later fade. But there was one great lasting expression of those aspirations, which was to continue for many years, leaving traces visible even today: the Gardner A. Sage Library.

From its beginning, Sage Library was conceived as a bold experiment based, as the Standing Committee put it, "upon foundations more liberal than those of kindred Institutions," and setting an "example that will be followed in other literary and theological centers."[22] The essence of Gardner Sage's vision was to assemble an ambitious collection of unrivaled excellence and at the same time to make it available it to a wide public beyond the seminary community itself. As Sage summarized his vision in a letter to his colleagues on the Standing Committee at the time, no fewer than ten thousand new books would be put on the shelves "during the coming two or three years," the building would be "kept open daily (except Sundays and holidays...) from early morning till evening," and its use is "to be extended to the whole Church and to the citizens of New Brunswick." Key to its operation would be a full-time librarian, whose job, "no sinecure," would be to supervise every aspect of the operation and who would not be a member of the faculty but rather directly accountable to the Standing Committee.[23] Thus, though the library would certainly serve the faculty and

15 Talbot W. Chambers (1819-1896), attended the seminary 1835-1836

students of the seminary, it would also have a life of its own beyond them—a life that, to be sure, would (so Sage strongly believed) do them honor.

The faculty apparently objected to such a policy at first, worrying that open public access to the library would hinder its use by faculty and students. Professors also objected more specifically to being denied keys to the new building—a policy intended, it would appear, to support the librarian's unilateral supervision of library use. In their protest they adduced their own comparison with other seminaries. "There is probably not a Seminary in the Country," wrote the faculty, "where each Professor has not his key to the books of the Institution."[24] In this matter the superintendents felt obliged to "affectionately" request the committee to provide the keys to the professors. Apparently the committee complied. But on the broader question of open access Sage stood his ground, being, as he put it, "fully convinced that with proper management naught but imaginary difficulties need arise with regard to its interference with the Seminary use." And he made an offer very attractive to everyone. If his plan for the library was adopted, he promised to "for the present, pay the salary of the Librarian in charge, together with the necessary current expenses for heating cleaning, etc.," and then to "endow it with a sum of money, the interest on which shall be sufficient to meet all these expenses annually"; in addition he promised a ten thousand dollar endowment to support acquisitions for the collection.[25]

Sage's vision for the library guided it for many years, and well past his own death. In the first several years, a joint committee of faculty members and scholarly alumni, chaired by Talbot Chambers of the Collegiate Church of New York (who was also a member, with Prof. John De Witt, of the American Standard Version translation committee, the worktable of which, a gift to the seminary in 1886, still stands in the library), made annual reports listing some of the new acquisitions (many of them multivolume foreign-language works) that appear calculated to impress upon the church the depth and seriousness of the collection.[26] And acquisitions increased steadily; in 1911, by which time the superintendents were regularly alerting the synod that more library space would be needed, the collection comprised fifty thousand volumes in a building designed for forty thousand.[27]

The person most responsible for keeping Sage's vision alive was the librarian, John C. Van Dyke. He came as a short-term library assistant in 1878 but stayed on, was appointed librarian in 1887, and remained in the position until his death in 1932. A man of wide interests, an author, and an art historian in his own right, he served concurrently as professor of art history in Rutgers College from 1891 to 1929. It was he who assembled the collection of faculty portraits that until recently hung in the library. He was frequently cited by the superintendents for his work as librarian, and, in 1891, the synod approved the construction of a residence for him on the campus (on George Street) as it had done for the faculty.[28]

Becoming "Eastern"

If in the seminary was staking out a place for itself in the world at large in the late decades of the nineteenth century, it was also finding itself in a new position within its own denomination, for now it was no longer the Reformed Church's only seminary. In 1866 the General Synod gave permission for "theological instruction" to be established at Hope College in Holland, Michigan, among the new Dutch immigrant communities of the Midwest, and the following year it elected a professor of theology to be based at Hope, with the same authority of office as the professors at New Brunswick. From these beginnings, a full-fledged theological seminary developed, with its own Board of Superintendents, known from 1885 as the "Western Theological Seminary."

The establishment of a second seminary meant that New Brunswick was no longer "the Theological Seminary of the Reformed Dutch Church," a phrase which previously had not just been a descriptor but actually served as its very name, insofar as it had one. In the synod minutes and elsewhere, it now begins to be denoted usually as "the Theological Seminary at New Brunswick," and, rarely, as "the New Brunswick Theological Seminary." Much later, in the twentieth century, the latter phrase became the normal title, though only *de facto*; to my knowledge, no official naming has ever taken place.

The relationship of the eastern and western (i.e., midwestern) sections of the church became a com-

16 *Sydney Noe, assistant to Van Dyke, ca. 1915. Noe became a distinguished scholar of numismatics.*

A Face to the World, 1850–1920

17, 18   Original interior of the Gardner A. Sage Library and the interior of the expanded building, ca. 1980.

plex one, in which New Brunswick Seminary had a major role from the outset. There was much cooperation; the eastern churches, which had always been New Brunswick Seminary's constituency, had welcomed the midwestern Dutch immigrants enthusiastically from their first arrival in the late 1840s, had provided much financial support for their institutions, and several early faculty members at Western Seminary as well as at Hope College had studied at New Brunswick. But tensions also emerged between the two regions, and the seminaries tended to become focal points of these.[29] Already in 1867 the superintendents at New Brunswick lamented the loss of half of the junior class "by the action of the last General Synod, allowing the Western students to study Theology in Hope College."[30] And when, ostensibly because of financial exigency, the General Synod suspended the theological institution at Holland in 1877 (a suspension that lasted until 1884), there was a general outcry in the West, where a writer in the newspaper *De Hope* attributed the action to "some in the East who have been jealous

19   John Charles Van Dyke (1861-1931)

of the establishment and growing of Hope College."[31]

The regionally representative structure of the national Reformed Church generally mediated and accommodated the sectional suspicions and rivalries between East and West. But there were deeper tensions, which, though slower to appear in full force, were harder to accommodate. These had to do with differences of theological disposition, which reflected the respective histories of the eastern and western churches. The westerners had belonged to the so-called "Secession" in the Netherlands that had resisted perceived encroachments upon the integrity of Reformed faith and practice by the cultural influences of post-Napoleonic Europe. They attended to the *purity* of the church with a force and urgency that felt strange to those in the East, where the church's formation in the period of the American Revolution had occurred in broad harmony with the birth of American republican institutions and had made them less attuned to such danger. The differences came fully into the open in the controversy over the General Synod's refusal in 1880 to take action to exclude Freemasons from church membership, a refusal that triggered the departure of many of the midwesterners from the RCA.

The difference of disposition between East and West tended also to reinforce emerging affinities, in the two regions respectively, in the controversies over "modernism" (i.e., broadly, the conflicts over whether and how Christianity should accommodate itself to the scientific age) that were to fracture American Protestantism in the late nineteenth and early twentieth centuries. The East, though still seeing itself as conservative in the broader scheme of things, tended to exhibit more openness to new strains of theological thinking that potentially challenged the older orthodoxies. And more than once New Brunswick faculty were the ones to exhibit the tendency. We find the first prominent example

20 *John De Witt the younger (1831-1906), class of 1842, faculty 1863-1892*

in a polite but serious debate that appeared in print in 1892–1893 between the recently retired New Brunswick professor John De Witt and the Western Seminary professor Egbert Winter (himself a New Brunswick alumnus, from 1863). De Witt located the "inspiration" of scripture within the biblical writers' understanding, i.e., within their "discernment" of what God imparted to them, the truth of which was then, he argued, subject to evaluation on the basis of its conformity to the truth personified by Christ.[32] Winter, in response, argued for a notion of the infallible truth of the biblical words themselves, which

African Americans

In 1877, the faculty's report to the Board of Superintendents includes reference to "Islay Walden and John H. Bergen, colored young men, members of the Second Church of New Brunswick," who are "seeking the ministry, with a view of laboring among their own people."[34] The report goes on to say that the two men have been attending the seminary for the previous year, and it recommends their official admission to the school.

Walden and Bergen were the first two African Americans whose attendance at the seminary is clearly documented.[35] They both graduated in the class of 1879, and both were then licensed and ordained by the Classis

21 Egbert Winter (1836-1906), class of 1863

he presented as a position more consistent with traditional Reformed orthodoxy than the views of his New Brunswick counterpart.[33] This is not the last instance of a church leader in the West taking a stance in response to what he perceived to be coming from New Brunswick.

Thus fault lines established themselves between East and West, which underlay tensions in the Reformed Church at the time and indeed have continued to do so. But it is important to note that the regions have mutually influenced each other in many productive ways and that New Brunswick Seminary has had a long tradition, extending to the present, of distinguished graduates who have come from the midwestern region of the church and thus have received their formation in both regions.

22 Islay Walden (1843-1884), class of 1879

23 John Bergen (d. 1893), class of 1879

of New Brunswick.[36] Walden became the founding pastor of a Congregational church under the auspices of the American Missionary Society in Randolph County, North Carolina, before his death in 1884.[37] Bergen, who was blind, ministered in Georgia, eventually joined the Southern Presbyterian Church, and died in 1893.[38]

Though of Bergen we know little of a personal nature, of Walden we know quite a lot, and he appears as a remarkable figure. He published two books of poems, the best of which still impress with their combination of simple directness, precise prosody, and emotional force.[39] The introductions to these volumes, one written by an anonymous friend, the other by the Reformed Church minister and New Brunswick alumnus William J.R. Taylor of Newark (father of Graham Taylor, on whom see below), tell Walden's story as they heard it from him. He was born into slavery in North Carolina; as a freedman after the Civil War, though his eyesight was poor he managed to walk all the way to Washington, D.C., where he supported himself in part by selling his poems on the street and established Sunday schools for indigent African American children. Then, trekking north through Pennsylvania and New Jersey, he eventually came to New Brunswick, where the Second Reformed Church gave him financial aid to return to Washington to attend Howard University and afterward to come back to New Brunswick to enroll at the seminary. In his time at the seminary he again organized a school for indigent children, which he described in a surviving letter as consisting of "60 odd scholars most of which were gathered from the streets" of New Brunswick, with "professors and students" from the seminary engaged to help in the enterprise.[40]

Over the next few decades, several other African American students attended the seminary. One of these, Archie G. Young, was pastor of the Ebenezer Baptist Church in New Brunswick at the time of his enrollment at the seminary as a special student in 1890–91. Another, Joseph De Cross Virgil, class of 1918, was a pastor in the African Methodist Episcopal Zion (A.M.E.Z.) Church. The others were all pastors of Mt. Zion African Methodist Episcopal (A.M.E.) Church in New Brunswick at the time of their study and subsequently served in other A.M.E. churches: Junius G. Ayler, class of 1886; Jordan Henry Christmas, class of 1904; Charles G. Collins, class of 1912; and John W. P. Collier, class of 1918.

World Mission

Missions continued to have a prominent place in the life of the seminary throughout the nineteenth

A Face to the World, 1850–1920

lands have gone from it [i.e., the society]" and that "a pastor who has once been a member of this Seminary and Society can hardly be conceived of, as indifferent to the claims of Foreign Missions."[41]

To survey all the New Brunswick graduates in foreign fields would beyond the scope of the present narrative,[42] but I will mention here a few whose contributions have been particularly significant.

One of the many graduates of the period who served as Reformed Church missionaries in the Amoy (South China) field (see part 1) was Abbe Livingston Warnshuis of the class of 1900, who went there upon his graduation and stayed until 1920. Afterward he became a leader in the movement of international cooperation among missionaries that the great Edinburgh Missionary Conference of 1910 had generated—first, as a member of the Chinese branch of the Continuation Committee

24 John W. P. Collier (1883-1971), class of 1918

century and well into the twentieth.

There continued to be graduates who became foreign missionaries. These accounted for about 7 percent of the graduates in the period from the 1830s through the 1910s (79 out of 1,054). But though they were a relatively small group in absolute terms, they held a disproportionate importance for the institution, constituting a point of great pride. Thus David Demarest in his historical discourse at the seminary's centennial celebration in 1884 called attention to the Society of Inquiry in particular as having cultivated interest in "every phase of the Missionary work" over time, such that that "some of the best Missionaries who have lived and died in heathen

25 Abbe Livingston Warnshuis (1857-1958), class of 1900

for that work from 1920 to 1925, and then from 1925 until 1942 as an executive (co-secretary) of the organization into which the Continuation Committee itself had evolved, the International Missionary Council. This council was one of the most important ecumenical organizations of the twentieth century, eventually (1961) becoming part of the World Council of Churches. Warnshuis had a major role in the formation of the relief organization Church World Service after World War II.[43] Warnshuis also, in retirement in the 1950s, served the seminary as its treasurer from 1946 to 1953.

The seminary also produced missionaries who served in the Reformed Church's mission in South India, the so-called Arcot Mission. Among the graduates were remarkable missionary families. One of these was the Scudder family, no fewer than ten of whom attended New Brunswick Seminary between 1855 and 1897, eight of them serving in the Arcot Mission for at least part of their careers. These were some of the sons and grandsons of the New York physician, John Scudder, and his wife, Harriet. They were Reformed Church members who served from 1819, first in Ceylon and then in India under the auspices of the American Board of Commissioners for Foreign Missions, before the founding of the Arcot Mission by three of their sons, including Jared Scudder of the class of 1855.

The other family of note was the Chamberlains. Jacob Chamberlain, who graduated from the seminary in 1859 and received his medical degree the same year, served in the Arcot Mission until his death in 1908. He was a remarkable polymath, active on the mission field not only as a physician and evangelist but also as a linguist of the Telugu language and an advocate of ecumenical cooperation among missionaries in India, as well as the author of books that popularized Indian missions to an American audience.[44] Two of Jacob's sons, William

26 Jared W. Scudder (1830-1910), class of 1855

of the class of 1886 and Lewis of the class of 1891, went back to India after graduation as missionaries before eventually returning to America. William became a long-term secretary of the RCA Board of Foreign Missions, and Lewis became an executive with the American Bible Society.

Another graduate of this period, Horace Grant Underwood of the class of 1884, became a pioneer missionary in Korea and a figure of great importance in the formation of a vibrant Protestant Christian tradition there. Underwood enrolled in the seminary in 1881, the same year that William A. Mabon, who had been Underwood's pastor and mentor in the Reformed church in New Durham, New Jersey, became professor of didactic

A Face to the World, 1850–1920

27 Samuel M. Woodbridge (1819-1905), class of 1841, faculty 1857-1901, and Jacob Chamberlain (1835-1908), class of 1859. Photograph ca. 1900.

28 Horace Grant Underwood (1859-1916), class of 1884

29 First structure (1887) of the Saemoonan Presbyterian Church, Seoul, founded by H. G. Underwood

and polemic theology. As Mabon had been distinguished as a planter of churches, so indeed would Underwood be. He arrived in Korea in 1885 under the auspices of the Presbyterian Board of Foreign Missions (the RCA board having lacked the funds to send him) and served there until shortly before his death in 1916. Like Jacob Chamberlain, Underwood stands out for the breadth of his contributions—pastor, evangelist, translator, and writer on mission themes, he also did much to build institu-

30 William A. Mabon (1822-1892), class of 1854, faculty 1881-1892

JAMES CANTINE   J. G. LANSING   S. M. ZWEMER
THE FOUNDERS OF THE ARABIAN MISSION
AS THEY APPEARED TWENTY-FIVE YEARS AGO. THE CENTRAL FIGURE, PROFESSOR LANSING OF THE NEW BRUNSWICK THEOLOGICAL SEMINARY, WAS NEVER ABLE TO GO TO THE FIELD AND HAS SINCE DIED

31 James Cantine (1861-1940), class of 1889; John G. Lansing (1851-1906), class of 1877, faculty 1884-1898; Samuel M. Zwemer (1867-1952), class of 1890

tions, founding the Korean YMCA and Chosun Christian College, which was to grow into Yonsei University.[45]

Less than a decade after Underwood, two other graduates of the seminary also became pioneers in a new mission field. As students, James Cantine of the class of 1889, who had grown up on a farm in Ulster County, New York, and Samuel Zwemer of the class of 1890, a pastor's son from Michigan, were deeply influenced by their Old Testament professor, John G. Lansing, himself an alumnus of the school (class of 1879) who had grown up in a missionary family in Syria and had a passion for mission to the Islamic world. "Through his class in the study of Arabic, and later in a little weekly prayer meeting for divine guidance," Cantine later wrote, they gradually came to know "that it was God's willed that we should offer ourselves for work in Arabia."[46] They then established, in the summer of 1889, the "Arabian Mission," an independent and (as they put it) "undenominational" organization supported by funds they themselves raised (though within a few years it came within the sponsorship of the RCA Board of Foreign Missions). They soon began their work, at first in Basra, and then in several locations on the Arabian Peninsula, laying the foundation for a Christian presence and witness in the Arab Muslim world that would find expression especially through medical and educational institutions and eventually through initiatives in interfaith understanding.[47]

The Arabian Mission Hymn

SING OF JESUS. 8s & 5s.

There's a land long since neglected,
There's a people still rejected
But of truth and grace elected,
　　In His love for them.

Softer than their night winds fleeting,
Richer than their starry tenting,
Stronger than their sands protecting,
　　Is His love for them.

To the host of Islams leading,
To the slave in bondage bleeding,
To the desert dweller pleading,
　　Bring His love to them.

Through the promise on God's pages,
Through His work in history's stages
Through the Cross that crowns the ages,
　　Show His love to them.

With the prayer that still availeth,
With the power that prevaileth,
With the love that never faileth,
　　Tell His love to them.

Till the desert's sons now aliens,
Till its tribes and their dominions,
Till Arabia's raptured millions,
　　Praise His love of them.

Prof. J. G. Lansing, 1889.

32 The Arabian Mission Hymn

The interest in foreign missions was indeed a constant through the period. But in this as in other aspects of the seminary's life, change manifested itself in a widened awareness of contexts beyond those of the Reformed Church and its own missions. Thus, in 1880 the Society of Inquiry, which in previous decades had tended to focus its debates and intelligence-gathering mostly on Reformed Church missionaries and mission policy,[48] now hosted, with the faculty's strong support, the first convention of the Inter-Seminary Missionary Alliance. It then sent delegates annually to the alliance's conventions, until in 1898, at a time when it included representatives from twenty-six denominations, the organization became the Theological Committee of the Student Division of the YMCA, of which the society then also eventually became an affiliate.[49] And in 1889, with funds donated by an elder from Syracuse, N. F. Graves, the faculty began a tradition of inviting speakers from many Protestant traditions to give the so-called Graves Lectures on missions every year—a tradition that endured, with few gaps, until at least 1933[50] and brought to campus such major ecumenical mission leaders as John R. Mott, Robert Speer, and J.H. Oldham.

The Gospel and Society

The last decades of the nineteenth century and the first decades of the twentieth saw some new Protestant theological responses to pressing social issues, especially concerning labor, industrialization, economic justice, and poverty, most notably in the movement called the "social gospel." Though New Brunswick Seminary is not known as one of its major centers, the movement had some resonance in the seminary's history.

On the faculty, it was Ferdinand Schenck whose teaching and writing most closely reflected social dismissed as "esoteric" or "speculative."⁵¹ Still, like Rauschenbusch and others in the movement, Schenck decried the inadequacy of Christian preaching that addressed only individuals and their personal conversions, and he had a strong sense of human sinfulness as not a matter of the individual human heart only, but as a systemic reality in the structures of society. Thus he questioned the morality of laissez-faire economics and saw the relation between labor and capital, and the regulation of industry, as matters of fundamental ethical importance for Christians. "The supply and demand theory of political economy," he wrote, "is not so wise as the 'Thou shalt not steal' of God."⁵²

Among graduates of the school, Graham Taylor of the class of 1873 (a year, that is, after Schenck) was himself a major social gospel figure. Taylor's roots at New Brunswick were deep; his father and grandfather had both graduated from the school (in 1822 and 1844 respectively), and he married Leah Demarest, daughter of the professor David Demarest. After serving a Reformed Church pastorate in rural Hopewell, New York, he accepted a call in 1880 to a Congregational church in urban Hartford, Connecticut, and became engrossed in the challenges of urban ministry. On the conviction that the message of salvation was a social message—as he put it in his diary, "no less, but not only, is the one soul to be sought and saved, but the world itself. And the world as the divinely constituted order of human life and relationships is to be won back to what it was made and meant to be—the Kingdom of the Father."⁵³ He then became a pioneer teacher and advocate of "social Christianity" at Hartford Seminary and from 1892 at Chicago Theological Seminary. There, with his wife, he also founded a settlement house, Chicago Commons, in a high-poverty area of the city, where he lived with family.

33 Graham Taylor (1851-1938), class of 1873

gospel concerns. The son of a Reformed Church minister, Schenck graduated from the seminary in 1873, and after several pastorates, became professor of practical theology in 1899, remaining in that position until he retired in 1924. He wrote prolifically and taught sociology as well as the more traditional topics of pastoral theology. Unlike Walter Rauschenbusch, the theologian most closely identified with the social gospel, Schenck did not attempt to construct a full-fledged theology centered on a notion of a "social" as distinct from "individual" salvation, nor did he share the "liberal" tendency of Rauschenbusch and others in the movement to prioritize the teachings of Jesus over traditional Protestant confessional stances

Another great advocate of "social Christianity" who graduated from New Brunswick Seminary was A.J. Muste, of the class of 1909. After several years of pastoral work in New York City and then in Massachusetts, Muste became a labor leader and social activist, one of the major voices for Christian pacifism in the twentieth century and a close friend and supporter of Bayard Rustin and other African American Civil Rights leaders.[54] Though in his post-seminary years he moved away from the traditional Reformed orthodoxy he had encountered at New Brunswick, he was asked back to the seminary repeatedly through the 1930s and 1940s to give short courses and individual lectures.

The Seminary and the Synod

In the decades around the turn of the twentieth century, the seminary's relationship to the Reformed Church's General Synod was changing, if subtly. The seminary still stood as the institutional manifestation of that office of professor that had been a function of the church's very identity from its beginning, and as such it was still an organ of the synod. But inevitably, given the developments we have considered here—and no doubt also the increasing size and complexity of the synod's overall program and responsibilities—the synod was also now recognizing the seminary's discreteness as an institution that had some responsibility for itself and that was guided in part by its own norms. Such recognition was perhaps implied already in 1883 by the synod's Board of Direction (executive committee) when it advised against a practice of bailing the seminary out from financial difficulty (in this case to supplement the salaries of professors) on the grounds of a wise policy followed by "many of the learned institutions of the country" to cultivate and rely on endowments created by their own benefactors, a policy that the seminary likewise should be following.[55] And indeed, after the report in 1898 of a "special committee on the finances of the seminary at new Brunswick," which lamented the insufficiency of the endowment and noted "that there are scarcely any living who have ever contributed a dollar for the Seminary's support"[56]—the age of Suydam and Sage being a thing of the past— the special committee became, in effect, a permanent committee, which reported annually to the synod for almost two decades on its efforts to increase the endowment. These efforts were slow and halting but eventually successful in raising the funds adequate to establish a sixth professorship.[57] Also in these years, the synod's method of electing professors changed. In con-

34 Abraham J. Muste (1885-1967), class of 1909

35 Faculty and students, 1899 or 1900. Faculty (first row, beginning fourth from left): Ferdinand S. Schenck (1845-1925), class of 1872, faculty 1899-1924; John H. Gillespie (1858-1924), class of 1885, faculty 1898-1923; Samuel M. Woodbridge; John H. Raven (1870-1949), class of 1894, faculty 1899-1939; and John P. Searle (1854-1922), class of 1878, faculty 1893-1922.

trast to the old method of nominating candidates from the floor of synod, from 1895 onward nominations were to be made in advance by classes; and then, from 1908, the Boards of Superintendents of the respective seminaries were to nominate the candidates (as is still the case today)—the rationale being, as an overture to the synod on the subject had put it in 1906, that "the members of Synod are often without [the necessary] information and have neither time nor facilities for securing same during the sessions of Synod."[58] Similarly, in 1894 the venerable question of whether and in what circumstances students should be allowed to preach, which had been of perennial concern of the synod in the early nineteenth century but only rarely discussed after 1860, was summarily "remitted to the control of the Faculties of the Seminaries."[59]

By the end of the period considered in this chapter, there was another change on the horizon in the relation between the synod and the seminary, a change that would have far-reaching implications in the years to come. In the very years when the special committee on the seminary's finances was reporting its very modest if steady progress in raising endowment, the synod was heavily promoting a program of "systematic beneficence" that encouraged congregations to remit contributions to the synod for the work of the "Boards and Funds" of the church, distributing them by percentage among the Boards of Domestic and Foreign Mission, Education, and Publication, and the Funds for Widows, and Disabled Ministers and Church Building. These efforts had great success; the Board of Foreign Missions, for example, which had received $120,000 from the churches in 1899 was receiving $325,000 by 1914. The seminaries were not included in the scheme, presumably because, having their own unique and ancient status in relation to the synod, they were neither "boards" nor "funds." But it must have seemed to some, at least, that the seminaries were being left behind, and the "Progress Campaign" inaugurated in 1918 with the goal of increasing the churches' beneficent giving to one million dollars per year included the seminaries in its budget.[60]

$\alpha\varpi$

This conceptual inclusion of New Brunswick Seminary in the denomination's overall efforts at fundraising was a small move, and hardly significant in itself. But in retrospect, we can see it as anticipating a larger change. For over the course of the twentieth century the seminary would inch away from its old status as a constituent element in the church, to become *one of the church's programs*, to be considered and evaluated like the others.

PART THREE

Ends and Means, 1920–1973

By the 1920s, a sea change was under way in New Brunswick Seminary's relationship to the Reformed Church. To be sure, the seminary's basic task or mission remained as it had been: to prepare students for ministry in the Reformed Church in America. But the General Synod was beginning to see the seminary less as a necessary constituent of itself, embedded in its very structure—as had been the case from the beginning—and more as a contingent instrument for purposes that could in theory be fulfilled in some other way. Accordingly, the question of the nature of "theological education" in the abstract would come to be a matter for discussion in its own right, logically prior to the question of how, or indeed whether, the church would support its existing seminaries. And accordingly the seminary—especially from 1923 when the office of president was established—took on the new responsibility of explaining itself, to demonstrate its worth to the church's discerning eye and also to find its own financial support. In the process, the school acquired a certain self-awareness and purposiveness that, by the 1960s, issued in ambitious planning for the future, and that, as denominational discussions of theological education took their course, would also eventually lead to a broadening of the seminary's mission to reach beyond the Reformed Church itself.

The Plan of 1923

A change in the relationship between the seminary and the General Synod begins to be apparent in the events that led up to the synod's adoption of a new plan for the seminary in 1923. The plan had been proposed by a committee formed the previous year to "consider the condition of our seminaries."

The synod's immediate concern in forming that committee had been the fact that both New Brunswick and Western were "badly hampered by lack of teachers and equipment" and as a result in danger of being "less effective than" the seminaries "of our sister denominations."[1] This was the familiar complaint of underfunding, coupled with the familiar comparative awareness of oth-

1   Front entrance to Hertzog Hall, ca. 1920s

er seminaries. But there was also something new about this committee's assignment: it was to consider not simply how the seminaries could be better provided for, but also whether the seminaries, as they currently existed, were the best means of providing the church with ministers. Was it necessary to maintain both institutions? Were they doing their job? How might they do it better? These were new questions for the synod to ask.

It soon became clear that these questions had touched a nerve in the church, especially as they applied to New Brunswick Seminary. New Brunswick, in particular, was not attracting students; as the committee's final report to the synod would put it, the "Church, and particularly the Eastern section of our Church"—New Brunswick's region—"has for some reason or other lost its former vital contact with the Seminaries. The erstwhile keen interest in these institutions, so pleasingly evident, is no longer found." The number of RCA students for ministry is "alarmingly small," and—what was particularly alarming—"even of that comparatively small number not a few pursue their studies in seminaries other than our own."[2] In the extensive discussion that appeared in the pages of the denominational weekly, the *Christian Intelligencer and Mission Field*, during the year 1922–23 when the committee was doing its work, the Vassar professor and Reformed Church minister William Bancroft Hill saw that the problem was precisely the seminary's lack of resources, "compared with such a highly equipped institution as, for example, Princeton."[3] Another writer, Lawrence French, a 1920 New Brunswick graduate who was then serving as the YMCA secretary at Rutgers, went further. The seminary's academic standards were too low, he said, and he announced that for this reason the "Seminary is even now about to be deserted by some of its most promising" students, who are "seeking a training for the ministry that will most adequately prepare them for their task."[4]

So there was a widespread perception that New Brunswick was falling behind. But we should not take this perception as a simple evaluation of quality. For alongside, or rather underneath, the doubts expressed about New Brunswick's adequacy was concern about a *theological* issue that had been finding its best-known expression in the "fundamentalist-modernist" controversies that so deeply divided American Protestantism at the time but which also, in less extreme ways, pervaded the daily life of the churches. That was the question of how and to what extent the Christian faith must adapt itself to lack of relevance to the "modern minister" and proposed a major change in the curriculum. Systematic theology, which was, he said, "the all dominating department," should be relegated to "the place to which it properly belongs," namely within the study of "religious thought and life"—i.e., classifying it (we gather) not as the exploration of revealed truth but as an instructive record of human religiousness.[5] The lion's share of the curriculum, then, should be given to "practical" and "experimental" (i.e., experiential) subjects such as preaching, Christian education, and field work.[6]

The other faculty voice in the discussion was that of the Reverend John H. Gillespie, who had been Berg's predecessor as professor of New Testament and then had continued to teach courses at the seminary until 1921. Gillespie quoted James Burrell, former synod pres-

2 J. Frederic Berg (1871-1958), class of 1895, faculty 1904-1917

the conditions of modernity. One suspects, in fact, that what French was really critiquing was not the seminary's academic shortcomings per se but what he saw as its theological backwardness.

This critique seems to have come particularly from eastern sources, and it appeared more explicitly (in the course of the newspaper discussion) in two articles by writers with teaching experience at New Brunswick itself. One of these was J. Frederic Berg, grandson of Joseph Berg, the professor who had served the seminary in the mid-nineteenth century (see part 2), who himself had been professor of New Testament from 1911 to 1917 but had resigned to take a pastorate in Brooklyn. Berg minced no words. He saw the problem at New Brunswick as a

3 John H. Gillespie

ident and minister of the Collegiate Church in New York, debunking any "claim that there is no right thinking religiously except in terms of three hundred years ago," and he pictured students' dismay at discovering the church's preference "to have her teachers remain static," that is, "stand still with the standards" [i.e., the RCA's constitutional Reformation-era standards of belief]. What the seminary needed to do to attract and keep students, Gillespie wrote, was to present the gospel "in terms of present-day thought" and to approach the Bible in ways that "run parallel with the advances already made in the physical and mental sciences."[7]

At the Synod of 1924 the committee produced a report that included a new constitutional plan for each of the seminaries. Surprisingly, perhaps, neither the report as a whole nor the plans individually attempted to address the pedagogical, institutional, and theological issues that had arisen, beyond affirming the valuable contributions of both seminaries (in New Brunswick's case the denomination's history being "quite unthinkable" without it) and dismissing the possibility, for the meantime anyway, of closing either one. Rather it proposed, in effect, that the seminaries solve their own problems, and to help them do so, the plans created new administrative structures for each school. Each was, for the first time, to have a president, and New Brunswick was to have a new twelve-person governing body called the Board of Managers (renamed in 1926 the Board of Directors), which would be chaired by the president and would take over most of the responsibilities of governance from the superintendents as well as from the former Standing Committee on Seminary Property.[8]

The implication seemed to be, for New Brunswick especially, that the creation of a chief administrative officer and a streamlined board, both with powers to act for the institution, would allow the seminary the chance to remedy the ills that faced it. No one needed to point out that the synod, to which the seminary was of course still accountable, would be watching to see how well it did. The synod accepted the report and approved the plans quickly, apparently with little debate. But the synod's action marks a major turning point in the seminary's history. The configuration of authority that had constituted it, in earlier days, as an extension of (as I have been terming it) the brotherhood of clergy had considerably faded, and—though to be sure the seminary would remain an object of loyalty and affection—the institution was now expected to plead its own cause.

President Demarest and the New Era

After the Plan of 1923 went into effect, the Old Testament professor John Howard Raven served for a time as acting president, and then, ostensibly at Raven's urging, the Board of Managers nominated William H.S. Demarest as president. The General Synod of 1924 elected him. Demarest served for a decade.

Demarest had had a long association with the seminary. He was the son of David D. Demarest, who served on the faculty as professor of pastoral theology and sacred rhetoric from 1865 to 1898. Born in 1863, William grew up on the New Brunswick's campus, graduated from Rutgers College in 1883 and the seminary in 1888. He served as a pastor in the Hudson Valley for thirteen years, first in Wallkill and then in Catskill, before becoming professor of church history at the seminary in 1901. In 1906 he was elected president of Rutgers College. He held that position until 1924, presiding over the considerable expansion of the college and its emergence as a major university. During his years as president he contin-

4   William H.S. Demarest (1863-1956), class of 1888, faculty 1901-1906, president 1925-1935

ued to be active in the affairs of the seminary, serving as a member of the Board of Superintendents from at least 1910 and sometime chair of the board's "reception committee" for admissions of the students from as far back as 1910. He also chaired the committee to choose a "sixth professor" once the money for that position had become available.

As a brilliant and experienced administrator who also knew the church well, Demarest skillfully addressed from the outset of his administration the issues of confidence that had underlain the synod's adoption of the Plan of 1923, especially those concerning academic reputation, morale, and church relations. (Demarest also had a role in addressing the related theological issues noted above—but that is a more complex matter, to which I will return below.) Throughout his presidency, he himself wrote the faculty reports to the superintendents—the substance of which would be repeated in the superintendents' reports to the synod—emphasizing matters that would enhance the seminary's reputation in the church. Thus he noted that faculty members were valued by other seminaries, who invited them to offer courses. Raven, for example, taught at Princeton Seminary for several years in the 1920s while retaining his job at New Brunswick. In 1926 he initiated an annual "Ministers' Conference" that served as a convocation for the academic year, and typically over a hundred ministers came to hear prominent speakers from many traditions (for instance, the Quaker theologian Rufus Jones in 1928). A particularly prized item of information, especially in light of the alleged low reputation of the seminary among students, appeared in Demarest's report of 1927. A "formal communication" had been received from the collective student body, expressing "high appreciation of the privilege they have received in their instruction by our several professors" and asking "that if possible some of the departmental lectures be given more publicity and wider service by their publishing in book form, thus adding at the same time to the prestige of our Seminary."[9]

As for academic matters: from 1926 all graduating students would earn the Bachelor of Divinity degree (by then the common degree for seminaries), conferred by Rutgers University to all graduating students. Up until this point, as present-day students are surprised to learn, the three-year seminary course at New Brunswick had not led to any academic degree at all, but only to the traditional Professorial Certificate. (There had been,

5   Students and faculty in the early 1930s. Faculty, front, from left: John W. Beardslee, Jr. (1879-1962), faculty 1917-1949; Theodore F. Bayles (1871-1952), class of 1898, faculty 1924-1941; Milton Hoffman (1886-1973), faculty 1925-1956; W.H.S. Demarest; John H. Raven; Edward S. Worcester (1876-1937), faculty 1923-1937; William A. Weber (1880-1968), faculty 1925-1950.

from 1893, the possibility of acquiring the B.D. through Rutgers on a "postgraduate" basis, for which the requirement had varied in the intervening years.[10]) Then in 1934, having been accredited by the New Jersey Board of Education, the seminary would grant the degree itself and no longer rely on the university.[11]

One innovation during the Demarest years that surely stood, in part anyway, as a response to the concerns that had surfaced in 1922–23 was a new attention to the "practical" matters of ministry. In 1926, at the end of his first full academic year as president, Demarest reported that "the students have had constant opportunity to preach among the churches and to do practical Christian work," under the direction of Theodore F. Bayles (himself of the class of 1898), a veteran pastor and sometime secretary of the Reformed Church's Board of Publication who had been elected professor of practical theology in 1924.[12] Bayles was in effect creating a field education program at the school, and its appearance in the 1920s stands as a particularly striking symbol of the changed relationship of the seminary to the synod, indeed of a subtle but significant change in the concep-

6 Students and faculty ca. 1921 on the steps of Suydam Hall. Faculty, in front, from left: John H. Gillespie; John W. Beardslee, Jr.; Ferdinand S. Schenck; John W. Beardslee, Sr.[?] (1837-1921), faculty 1917-1921; John P. Searle; Edward P. Johnson [?](1850-1924), faculty 1906-1924; John H. Raven.

tion of the school itself. For only a few decades earlier, as we have seen, both synod and faculty had considered "student preaching" to be an outright evil that violated a highly valued distinction between "student" and "minister." But now the faculty is presenting student preaching to the synod as a sign of the school's progress and relevance! Pretty much gone is any sense of the seminary as a liminal space for the sequestering of young men as they are being formed; it has become instead a practice-ground for their future exertions. Demarest's reports routinely describe Bayles's work and convey his statistics: in 1927, students conducted 402 "preaching services" in 41 churches in 31 classes; in 1930 the figure was 544 services in 57 churches in 20 classes.[13]

The Demarest years also saw new construction on the campus for the first time in several decades. There were two new structures. One of these was a new addition to the library, completed in 1929, the so-called "Wessels Memorial Building" (consisting of the whole portion of library that lies to the north of the Great Hall), responding to the need for increased storage that had been first sounded in the reports of the Permanent Committee on Seminary Finances almost three decades earlier and funded by a bequest from the estate of Mary B. Pell. The other structure was the so-called "Missionary House," a duplex residence built in 1930 on the east side of the campus[14] for missionary families on furlough. The idea for acquiring or constructing such a building as a "service" of the seminary to the church, on recognition that the furloughing missionaries would often also be "graduate students," first appears in the minutes of the directors for 1926 and conforms to Demarest's overall policy of care to cultivate good relations with the denomination; it was funded by specially solicited donations.[15] The building served its intended function until 1963, when it was moved to the corner of Seminary Place and College Avenue to be used as faculty residences.[16]

All in all, under Demarest the school had an efficient central administration with purposes clearly envisioned and plans to carry them out, and it was solvent and attentive to its relations with the church. To be sure, by 1934, when Demarest retired, the Depression was hitting hard, and the directors reported to the synod "a difficult and not satisfactory year in the financial way," with income down by more than 30 percent and salaries reduced.[17] But even so, as the faculty report of 1935 put it, the "hopes" that Demarest's election had aroused in 1924 had been "more than realized by the accomplishments of the past decade."[18]

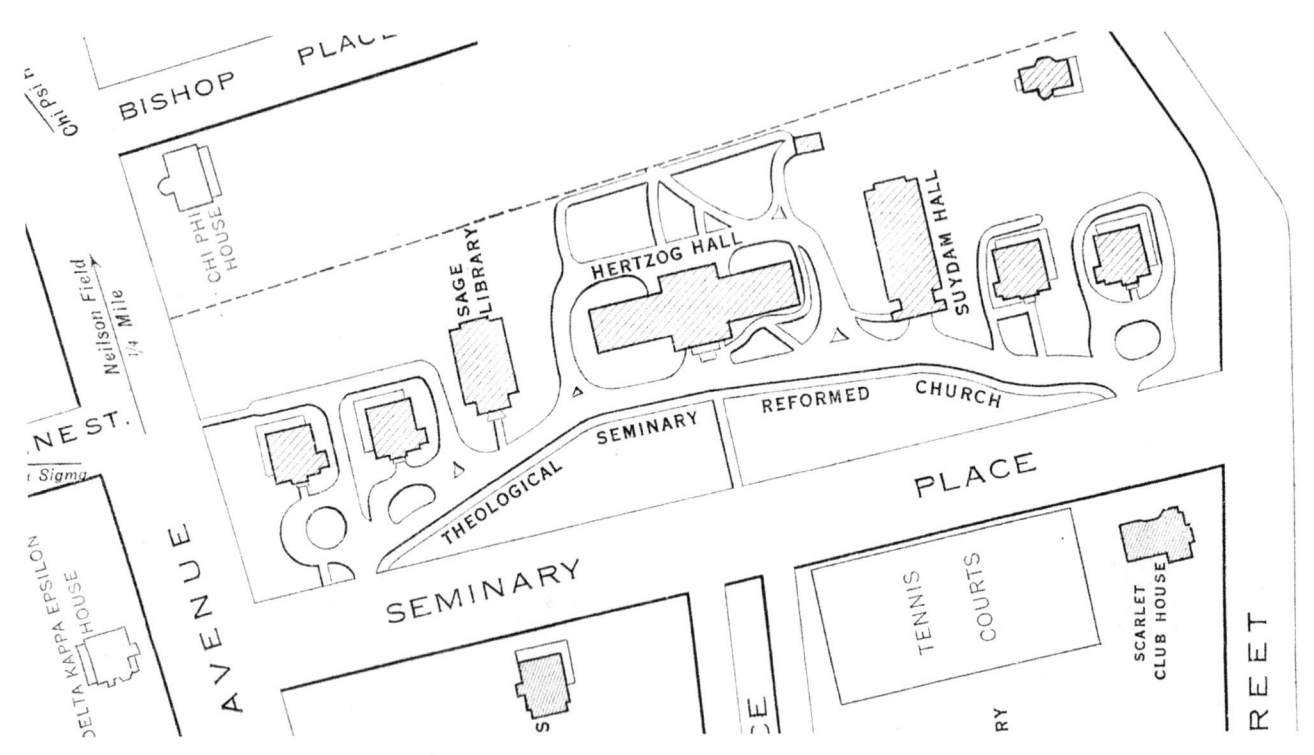

7   Plan of the campus, early twentieth century

The Election of Professor Worcester

In 1923, the same General Synod that adopted the new plans for the seminaries also elected, after several ballots and much debate, a new professor of systematic theology for New Brunswick— Edward Strong Worcester. Though Demarest at that moment was still at Rutgers and was not to become president of the seminary for another year and a half, he nonetheless chaired the superintendents' search committee that brought Worcester's name forward, and he gave the nominating speech at the synod, even though he was not a delegate. The election stands as an early event in the "Demarest era." It suggests how the theological aspect of the recent critiques of New Brunswick figured in the seminary's situation, and in Demarest's vision.

Worcester had had no previous direct connection with the Reformed Church in America. This was unprecedented in a professor elected by the synod. He had graduated from Hartford Seminary, then studied in Germany, and for twenty years had served Congregational churches in Wisconsin and New England. Demarest felt constrained to explain to the synod in his nomination speech that the committee had been unable to find RCA candidates who were willing to be nominated, and he assured them that Worcester came highly commended by distinguished persons well known in the denomination.[19]

8 Sesquicentennial Celebration of New Brunswick Seminary, in 1934, shortly before the retirement of President Demarest, who presided over the festivities. He is likely the figure seen in profile at the upper left corner of the photograph, receiving guests who have entered the Great Hall of the library through its front door.

9 Edward Strong Worcester

But the major controversial point about Worcester was his theology. In a memorandum to the superintendents, he had registered reservations about some statements in the denomination's constitutional Standards, that is, in the Heidelberg Catechism, the Belgic Confession, and the Canons of Dort, to which as a professor he would be required to subscribe. Specifically, for instance, he questioned whether scripture warranted the assertions that Adam had been initially sinless, or that Adam was the progenitor of all humankind, and he commented provocatively that the notion of our "guilt responsibility" for Adam's sin on account of our being "in the loins of Adam" is "a bit of the fanciful or allegorizing theology of the rabbinic period in Judaism and similar schools in Christianity, which is worse than meaningless to-day." He also had concerns about the language used by the Canons of Dort to define the doctrine of Election (although his views, it seems, were not Arminian), and he appeared to question whether scripture was inerrant in "all things" as distinct from "all things necessary to salvation" or "all things which constitute a rule of faith and practice."[20]

Worcester's reservations about the Standards elicited opposition to his election. A group of delegates at the synod, led by Gerrit Hospers, a pastor from the Classis of Rochester who hailed from Iowa and who as a member of the Board of Superintendents had dissented from the nomination, circulated a broadside that quoted from the candidate's memorandum to expose his views and rally resistance.[21] And though those who opposed Worcester did not win the day, the election aroused strong feelings. It would cause, over the following decades, what Howard Hageman has called a "fracturing" in the Reformed Church by fueling a persistent suspicion, especially in the Midwest, that the theological commitments of New Brunswick Seminary were unsound.[22]

What is important to note, however, is not so much the fact of Worcester's opponents as the conviction of his supporters. In a long letter to Demarest after the conclusion of the synod, Hospers described conversations during the synod with Professor Raven and with his fellow superintendents, all of whom tried to dissuade him from opposing Worcester, on the grounds of the "delicate situation in the Seminary" or the "seriousness of the situation" there, which the superintendents in particular spoke of "in terms of despair almost."[23] The discussions we have overheard in the *Intelligencer and Mission Field* suggest what that "situation" was —a combination of decreased enrollment, low morale, and generally a lack of confidence in the institution—and the contributions by Berg (who also was on the search committee for Worcester) and Gillespie to that discussion indicate how some well-placed people at New Brunswick diagnosed the problem; namely, that it was a matter of the seminary being perceived as irrelevant to modern life, as stuck in the past. In that light, Worcester must have symbolized a turnaround. The opposition no doubt had cause to conclude that a "liberal" or "modernist" tendency was at least implied in the support for Worcester. But the support for him is not to be understood in a narrow sense, as though the faculty and friends of the school were bent on defending his views on original sin or biblical inerrancy. It is doubtful, for instance, that Raven, a biblical scholar of conservative temperament, would have been completely of a mind with Worcester in these matters. And Demarest, when he heard that the content of the memorandum had been made public to the synod, wished the nomination had been withdrawn; clearly he did not want to fight about the content of the Standards.[24] What lay behind the solid support for Worcester within the seminary seems not so much a critique of the church's traditions of belief as a broader conviction that to recover its vitality the school had to focus less on the conservation of tradition *per se* and more on a direct encounter with the modern world. This, at least, seems to have been what the most of the seminary's leadership saw to be at stake in the election.

A look at the inaugural lectures of other figures who joined the faculty in the Demarest years, none of whose doctrinal views excited opposition, shows them nonetheless sharing that same wish for the seminary to focus resolutely on a Christian response to the needs of

10 Milton Hoffman teaching

the world in the present. Thus Bayles the practical theologian spoke in 1924 of the need of Christian people, under the influence of the ministry, to "feel the urge of Christ's message and the adaptability of that message to their own disturbed age";[25] Milton Hoffman the professor of church history in 1925 argued that the "past is alive in the present" and that "the touchstone of orthodoxy" is "a Christ-like spirit" rather the strict measure of a creed considered in itself;[26] and Weber the educator in 1926 declared that "we do not ignore the past and its wealth of knowledge….But in the work of the ministry today the emphasis is on the present highly complicated problems and needs" of the world.[27] The lectures share a common tone that is positive and engaged—the tone, in sum, of the Demarest era.

As for Worcester himself: he taught at the seminary until his death in 1937 and served also as associate librarian, taking over many of the functions of the then aged Van Dyke. Within the seminary community he was not a divisive figure but rather a teacher and colleague deeply respected by all for, in the words of Raven, "his great powers of mind and heart."[28]

Presidential Directions, 1935–1959

The seminary's decade under William Demarest set the agenda for the quarter-century (1935–1960) that followed his retirement. The fundamental thing was the enduring fact of the presidency itself, the legacy of the Plan of 1923: now a central administration shaped the life of the school by identifying its major tasks and devising strategies to accomplish them. Those tasks as Demarest had pursued them were to enhance the purposiveness and quality of the school's academic program, to maintain good relations with the Reformed Church in America and its churches, and accordingly to sustain a student body of a viable size. These, with variations in emphasis, remained the major tasks that the school pursued under the next three presidents as well—John W. Beardslee Jr., Joseph R. Sizoo (1947–52), and M. Stephen James (1942–59)— more or less successfully. For though finances, to be sure, were a constant concern, this was a time when New Brunswick stood as a stable and viable denominational seminary.

John W. Beardslee, Jr. served as president from 1935 to 1947. A scholar to the core, he had become professor of New Testament in 1917 and remained in that position in his years as president. Alongside the financial challenges that he and the directors addressed in the years of the Depression and World War II, the academic program occupied him particularly. Under his leader-

11 At the 175th anniversary of the seminary, in 1959: Mrs. Frances Beardslee; John W. Beardslee, Jr; M. Stephen James (see p. 68) holding the engraving printed at the time of the centennial (see p. 35); Wallace N. Jamison (see p. 76)

ship the old system of examining each class before the superintendents was changed so that from 1936 there were to be two examinations only: one comprehensive at the end of the middler year on all the work covered to that point, and then a set of senior essays which were to synthesize the student's skills and learning around stated themes. The faculty reports suggest that there was a continuing discussion of the question of the best form for exams to take.[29] An "honors" track was also instituted in 1936, in which approved students could do extra reading in a particular field; in 1937 three of these were reading "Origen, Athanasius, Chrysostom and the like."[30] By 1942 we find a policy in place requiring every senior to write a thesis.[31] Distinguished adjunct professors taught on a regular basis, including the social activist A.J. Muste (himself of the class of 1909), who taught courses in "social Christianity," and, at different times, George Buttrick and Norman Vincent Peale (who taught homiletics).[32] After Beardslee's resignation from the presidency in 1947, "to have more time to study," the superintendents' affectionate statement of appreciation made a particular point of crediting his "patient, tirelessly painstaking planning" as having led to a "Class A" accreditation by the Association of Theological Schools, "without notation"—which as the superintendents had been informed was the ATS's "highest classification, reserved for only a limited number of Seminaries."[33]

As for Sizoo and James, both of them had been veteran pastors before coming to the seminary—the nationally known Sizoo (of the class of 1910) in Washington D. C. and New York, and James in Albany (before joining the faculty in 1942)—and both focused the institution's energies on relations with the church, especially the local congregation. The great goal to "bring the seminary closer to the life of the Church," as Sizoo put it in his first meeting with the Superintendents,[34] was of course not new. However, at this time financial support from local churches became a central concern, indeed it became the main organizing principle of the seminary's church relations, which had not been the case earlier. The minutes of both the directors and the superintendents constantly register plans and efforts by the presidents, aided by board members and faculty, to bring the seminaries' needs before the local churches.

Already at the beginning of his presidency in 1947, Sizoo had the idea to "ask the churches to take a special offering for the Seminary" one Sunday a year, and this became rapidly established as "Seminary Sunday" every October. By 1951, a year before he resigned, Sizoo was reporting to the directors that "over one half of the churches" in the eastern synods were observing Seminary Sunday, that eighty-three churches had "increased their gifts" in the preceding year and twenty-one had "given for the first time," and that the churches were being challenged to contribute one dollar per member annually to the seminary.[35]

James, who became president in 1953, continued these efforts, and in 1959, the year he retired, the superintendents' report to the synod showed that church support had doubled under his leadership.[36] Also in James's time, the Women's Auxiliary was founded by several wives of faculty members—Marjorie James, Frances Beardslee, Eunice Vander Kolk, Julia Van Wyk—and two other church women, Ruth Mook of Metuchen

12 Joseph R. Sizoo (1885-1966), class of 1910, president 1947-1952, is here shown on a visit to wartime Korea in 1952, with American army chaplains and a Korean Pastor, Lee Eung Wha

and Gladys Vosseller of Somerville. The group has continued to the present, providing major support to the seminary in many ways, including the raising of scholarship money.[37]

Also under the administrations of Sizoo and James, the seminary conducted its first capital fund drive for purposes of repairs and construction on the campus. The goal of $150,000 in special donations, adopted in 1951 for what came to be called the "Modernization Fund," was modest by comparison to efforts in the following decade, and in fact the goal does not appear to have been finally met. But by 1957 enough had been raised for the razing of the faculty residence on the west end of seminary row (where Hoffman and family had lived until his retirement that year) and the building of a duplex faculty residence in its place.[38]

A New Confidence

The seminary's theological stance and how it was perceived continued to be part of the picture during

13   M Stephen James (1889-1973), faculty 1942-1959, president, 1953-1959

this time. A brief controversy in 1948–49 suggests what was changing theologically and what was not in the decades of institutional stabilization after Worcester's election.

The controversy concerned the inaugural lecture given by Hugh Baillie MacLean in 1948. MacLean, a Scotsman who had earned a doctorate at Union Seminary in New York and then had served in the Royal Air Force during World War II, began teaching at New Brunswick in 1947, was elected professor of Old Testament by the synod the following summer, and would be a beloved teacher at the school until his untimely death in 1959. His 1948 lecture was on the "relevance of the Old Testa-ment." In it he discussed, among other things, the biblical narratives of the conquest of "the Promised Land" with their implication that God had commanded the "ruthless extermination of peoples." He commented that in implying this, the writers "rewrote the history of Israel" in such a way that "it may have been falsified," but that they did so to express in their own context their sense of the danger of a "secularization of life and religion," a danger still to be feared in our present context—thus affording an example of the relevance of the Old Testament even when the text may be most troubling.[39]

When the denominational magazine, the *Church Herald*, published the lecture later that fall, MacLean's apparent questioning of the factuality of the biblical narrative raised alarms, especially in the midwestern region of the church, about his view of the inspiration and authority of the scriptures. At the Synod of 1949 there were overtures from thirteen classes, all from that region, requesting that MacLean explain himself, though there were also seventeen overtures, all from the East, that expressed support for MacLean personally and/or for the seminary. MacLean did explain himself, in a letter addressed to the president and superintendents and submitted to the synod. In it he affirmed his "loyalty to the doctrinal standards of the Reformed Church...without reservation," and explained that he did not deny the truth of the biblical narratives in question. By using the word "falsified," he meant only that the inspired writings used "historical facts...to vindicate a particular philosophy of history." The special synod committee appointed to review the matter expressed satisfaction with his statement and expressed "full confidence" in his election as professor the previous year.[40]

The controversy over MacLean was milder in substance than the controversy over Worcester a quarter century earlier, but the common denominator of the

14 Hugh Baillie MacLean (1909-1959), faculty 1948-1959

two incidents was that they exposed suspicion within the Reformed Church about New Brunswick Seminary's faithfulness to the Reformed standards. Clearly that suspicion was not going away. Moreover—even though MacLean, unlike Worcester, declared himself to adhere to the standards without scruple—the suspicion was not entirely without basis on the part of those who entertained it. That is, it was not merely a misunderstanding as MacLean's explanation may have construed it, since for many in the midwestern classes the notion that a biblical text could be in any sense the result of "falsification" undermined belief in the authority of scripture.

Though suspicion thus remained in the church, things had changed at New Brunswick itself since the time of Worcester's election. Gone was the sense of crisis and the feeling that a move in the modernist direction would be the school's saving. By the time of MacLean's lecture, the school displayed a confidence in its faculty and what now appears as a moderate theological stance, whereby the standards were not questioned, indeed were affirmed, but the encounter with modernity, and the notion that scripture should be read in the light of it, remain central. The attitude of confidence was apparent already in 1947, before MacLean had even arrived on campus, when, at their first meeting with Sizoo, the superintendents reacted to attacks recently made in print by Henry Bast, a pastor from Michigan, against eastern RCA institutions, especially New Brunswick Seminary, for fostering "liberalism." The superintendents disputed the truth of "statements...which indiscriminately allege the heretical teachings and thought emanating from the Seminary," and went on the offensive, decrying the "methods used" in such "unsubstantiated attacks," and unanimously passing a resolution to affirm the policy of appointing the "best qualified and available" faculty members "whether they are or are not members of the Reformed Church."[41] Even so, in these middle decades of the twentieth century the New Brunswick faculty followed the broad neo-orthodoxy of mid-century mainline Protestantism, typically affirming the substance of the confessional standards (i.e., rather than submitting them to the kind of critique that had caused controversy in Worcester's case) while also accepting the principles of the historical criticism of scripture—and, MacLean excepted (indeed unintentionally), avoided overt controversy in the Reformed Church.[42]

15 Among the few African American graduates during the middle decades of the century was Wilbur Washington (class of 1952), who would return to the seminary to teach homiletics and supervise field education from 1980 to 1995. He was elected the first African American president of the General Synod in 1991.

New Brunswick and Foreign Missions

From the 1920s onward, interest in foreign missions appears not to have been as conspicuous a theme in the seminary's life as it had been in the decades prior to the First World War. No doubt this reflects in part the shifting attitudes toward foreign mission in American Protestantism generally in the period, amid debates over its proper ends.[43] Yet the interest was still there. Though the Graves Lectures ceased to be a yearly event in the mid-1930s, missionaries and mission executives continued to visit the campus regularly to lecture and meet with students, there were regular courses on missions, and the Missionary House accommodated missionaries on furlough. Most importantly, there were still graduates who went out from New Brunswick to foreign fields. Indeed there were too many for all to be mentioned here, but I call attention to three who have been particularly well known: Walter de Velder of the class of 1935, who with his family served in China until 1950, when they were obliged by the Communist government to leave, and thereafter in the Philippines, Hong Kong, and Taiwan; John S. Badeau of the class of 1928, who served in the Arabian mission and later became an academic and a sometime U.S. ambassador to Egypt; and Edwin Luidens of the class of 1943, who also served in the Arabian mission and later became secretary of the Board of World Missions of the Reformed Church and a mission executive with the National Council of Churches.

The 1960s: The Shaking of the Foundations

We have seen that in the early 1920s, the Reformed Church, rather than simply assuming the existence of its seminaries as in the past, had begun for the first time to step back and ask the question how best to pursue the task of theological education, with the implication that some other means might be preferable, in theory anyway, to the seminaries as they stood. In the decades that followed, the question was rarely addressed directly, though it remained implicit, as the successive presidents and boards at New Brunswick (indeed like those at Western) kept their seminary focused on its task and attentive to its relations with the church—i.e., concentrated both on doing its job and on being seen doing its job. But then in the decade of the 1960s, the question of how to do theological education became explicit again, as the church asked once more whether two seminaries were necessary. The discussion would result in major consequences for New Brunswick Seminary.

Ends and Means, 1920–1973

16 Walter de Velder (class of 1935) served in China and Asia from 1929 to 1977

17 Henry Stout (class of 1868) served in Japan from 1869 to 1906

In contrast to the 1920s, this time the question of how best to do theological education did not arise because the seminaries were in any immediately perceptible decline. New Brunswick, in fact, embarked in the early 1960s on an ambitious campus plan and was meeting with success in fundraising. In fact, the question now came as much from within the seminary itself—indeed from very process of the campus planning—as from the church at large. Everyone involved shared the acute awareness of the challenges posed by a changing world that so characterized the decade of the 1960s and made planning for the future a high priority.

In 1959 Justin Vander Kolk, who had taught at the seminary since 1946 and had been professor of systematic theology since 1951, was elected president. He called immediately for a "master plan of campus development and Seminary promotion."[44] By October 1960 an ambitious plan was in place (though it would be revised repeatedly) that called for, among other things, new housing for faculty and for married students, a new classroom/administration building, a new chapel, and enlargement of the library.[45] By mid-1961, funding plans were also in place, which included the "United Synod Advance" capital fund initiatives conducted by the eastern regional synods, which envisioned at first a goal of $2.5 million, half of it in endowment (although the endowment portion soon disappeared from the plans).[46] In reporting these plans to the General Synod in 1961, the superintendents spoke optimistically.

> There is everywhere new evidence of the concern and interest of our churches. We are blessed with a vigorous and able faculty. The current enrollment of 68 is the largest in the history of our school. We are moving forward and we shall continue to move forward.[47]

18 Justin Vander Kolk (1906-1994), class of 1936, faculty 1946-1959, president 1959-1963

19, 20 The moving of the Missionary House

The fundraising proceeded successfully, and by the end of 1963 the first fruits of the plan were visible: a two-unit residence for faculty at 89 College Avenue had been constructed the previous year, the Missionary House became another two-unit faculty residence and was moved in mid-1963 from its original location behind Suydam Hall to the corner of Seminary Place and College Avenue, and the seminary had signed contracts for the married-students' dormitory to be opened in 1964 and named Scudder Hall (after the pioneer missionary John Scudder).[48]

The campus would continue to change in a major way after those beginnings, but the planning process took a new turn. In the spring of 1963, President Vander Kolk resigned—having, as Howard Hageman would recall, "little appetite for all of the details that would be involved in planning and constructing the new buildings"[49] after the overall plan had been conceptualized. His successor, Wallace N. Jamison, who had served from 1957 as professor of church history and from 1961 also as dean, appears to have been more comfortable with plans and details. It was Jamison who—in close association with Walter Gates, a layman who had come from the lumber business to become director of development in early 1963 and later served as business manager—took the lead in getting the boards to rethink their plans more radically. In a meeting in October 1964, the directors reviewed and began to question "some of the original assumptions" of the campus plan. In particular, they decided that the projection of student population (at least one hundred) had been excessive, given the size of the potential pool of candidates for ministry in the Reformed Church, and that "the practice of faculty and students, both married and unmarried, of living on the campus," should be reconsidered. Moreover, Rutgers University had expressed an interest in buying the campus, and a "quick calculation" showed the feasibility of using the newly available capital funds plus the proceeds of a campus sale to relocate and build a campus precisely suited to current needs. Consideration of that possibility in turn raised another, namely "the possibility of merger with" Western Theological Seminary.[50] By the end of that meeting, all options were on the table, and at the directors' request, in that same month of October 1964 the superintendents put all building plans on hold while other possibilities were considered.[51]

The decision opened a wide discussion about the future of the seminary. In January of 1965, the directors decided to postpone the decision about selling the campus and relocating the seminary, and as it turned out this option would not be very thoroughly explored.[52] The discussion focused rather on the possibility of merger with Western Seminary. The New Brunswick faculty, when polled for its opinion, opposed such a merger by a vote of 9–0. However, the superintendents, joined by the board at Western Seminary, still voted that month to ask the Permanent Committee on Theological Education—a committee that had been recently established by the General Synod to consider, among other things, the "new demands" on the seminaries "because of the growing diversity of the ministry, the increased complexity of the training required, plus the new disciplines appearing"—to consider the possibility of merger.[53] Though Jamison, who favored the idea of the merger,[54] chaired the committee, it reported that summer that it opposed the idea, but that "nonetheless, it is our judgment that there are more opportunities for more effective unification and coordination of theological education in the Reformed Church and that this should be a continuing concern of the seminaries, their boards and administrations and of this committee."[55] The synod adopted the report. So at that point there was at least a goal for continued planning—not merger but "unification and coordination," even if no one knew yet quite what this would mean.

The boards at New Brunswick Seminary decided that the decision against merger meant that they could go ahead with plans for developing the campus. In October 1965 the superintendents resolved that "we remain at the present site and develop this site...in the conviction that the Church in the East needs the Seminary to stand at the center of its life." Almost immediately they approved in principle a new plan to raze both Hertzog Hall and Suydam Hall and construct in their place a "multi-purpose building" containing "classrooms, offices, chapel, visual aids, etc."[56] Things then moved very quickly. Demolition of the old buildings began in March 1966, with Suydam Hall.[57] In April, the architect Arnold W.

New Brunswick Theological Seminary: An Illustrated History

21, 22 Demolition of Hertzog Hall

23 Construction of Scudder Hall

24 Zwemer Hall Chapel

25 Completed Scudder Hall

(Pete) Rose presented plans for a new, single-story multipurpose building, in what was described as a "new and dynamic" architectural style, featuring a circular chapel, and superintendents passed a motion "with no audible opposition" to begin construction in the fall of 1966 after the razing of Hertzog in the summer.[58] The building went up over the 1966–67 academic year and was dedicated in October of 1967 as Zwemer Hall, in honor of the missionary Samuel Zwemer of the class of 1890.

So the leadership at New Brunswick assumed the seminary would remain *where* it was, at least for the meantime. But that it would not remain *as* it was became clear as the Reformed Church began to work out what "unification and coordination" of its theological education might look like. The Synod of 1966 appointed a committee "to frame a plan for the creation of a single Board of Theological Education" in place of the boards of the individual seminaries, and to "present the plan to the General Synod of 1967." Moreover, when the plan was presented, it became clear that the creation of a single board was to be more than a coordinating effort between the two seminaries. It would be a body that would have the purpose of, in the words of the General Synod Executive Committee, "establishing a single theological Seminary for the Reformed Church in America."[59] So the idea of an outright merger had not disappeared after all. As the synod approached, the faculty and superintendents at New Brunswick issued a joint statement objecting that this was going too far, too fast.[60] But the measure passed.

A "Unified Administration" and a New Approach to Seminary Education

The merger of the boards of New Brunswick and Western Seminaries in 1967 into a single body—which in 1970 would be officially called the "Board of Theological Education" (BTE) of the Reformed Church—had an enormous effect on New Brunswick. For one thing, the seminary ceased to be an entirely discrete institution. For another, it made a bold change in the seminary's curriculum, that is, in what was taught and how.

By 1969 the merged boards had moved to create a "unified administration" to oversee both seminaries, and they requested the resignations of both presidents—Herman Ridder of Western and Wallace Jamison of New Brunswick (who after a sabbatical year became dean of Illinois College in Jacksonville, Illinois)—and then appointed Ridder "President of both seminaries." Ridder kept that job for two years. During that time he was present at New Brunswick only about four days per month, and it was Norman Thomas (class of 1944) who, leaving his pastorate in Albany that year to become dean of the seminary, took charge of the day-to-day administration of the school. Yet Ridder had all the authority of the president and exercised it in matters small and large, including the new curriculum, of which he remained chair of the "program design committee."[61]

That new curriculum was the great work of the newly connected seminaries. As the design committee (consisting of the two presidents, two faculty members from each school, and three board members) worked it out in 1968, influenced by the Association of Theological Schools' so-called "Curriculum for the 1970s" and using Gordon Kaufman of Harvard Divinity School as its consultant, the seminary's plan attempted to reconceive theological education as professional education.[62] As such it

26 Wallace N. Jamison (1918-2010), faculty 1956-1963, president 1963-1969

created a process to help the student to be formed, as a person, for the profession of ministry, instead of attempting, as in the past, to walk a precarious "tightrope" (as the committee put it) between being a "trade school" that taught skills, and being a "graduate school" that trained scholars. Such professional formation required students to exercise theological reflection on experience—and on engagement with the world around them at various sites—as a constant throughout, but it progressed, as the committee envisioned it, in two stages or "levels."

The first of these, called the "Christian identity level," in which students would learn "to live and act in the world with theological understanding," would be offered at New Brunswick in the first two years of the student's work toward the Bachelor of Divinity degree (which in 1971 was renamed, as in other seminaries, the Master of Divinity). The second, called the "professional ministry" level, in which they learned to "equip the church for her mission in the world, by exercising the skills of ministry," would be offered in a two-year residence (which could be extended or reduced according to the needs of the student) at Western.[63]

This new "Bi-Level Multi-Site" (BLMS) curriculum began operation in 1970–71, when the new students spent the first of two years engaging in the "Christian Identity Level" at New Brunswick. Most of the faculty took up the work with enthusiasm, including a new faculty member, Hugh Koops, who had transferred to New Brunswick from Western because his field, Christian ethics, was thought particularly pertinent to Level One.

27 Chapel in Zwemer Hall, as seen from the pulpit in the spring of 1985

28 This photograph from 1973-1974 shows a "core" group of students in the BLMS program (from the left, Robert McAndrews, Thomas De Vries, Richard Otterness, Paul Wesselink, Robert Hoffman), with their instructor Paul Fries (on the right), being sworn in as deputy police officers in the city of New Brunswick. They helped patrol the streets in uniform, their experience becoming the basis of their group's theological reflection.

The innovative aspects of the Level One work were the "historical-theological" courses, which were organized not by chronology or system but rather by "motifs" that served to place "the theological questions of the past... in relationship to the basic questions that we must ask in the present," and the so-called "Core" groups in which students and faculty would reflect in theological and personal terms on aspects of life in their immediate environment in the city of New Brunswick, and would "relate to people not usually found within the structures of the church." For example, the focus of Professor David Waanders' group the first year would be "the needs of young people, especially those of junior high age who have difficulty with school adjustment," and that of Professor Paul Fries would be the "youth culture" in the "university setting."[64] The results were promising. "For the first time," the BTE declared in its report to the Synod of 1971, "we have a program of theological education which allows a student to receive the best seminary education which the Reformed Church can offer. A new 'mix' has been created in the student body in which the old divisions and separations [between the seminaries]...fell away. It is admittedly a bold experiment but a most promising one."[65]

But in fact the bold experiment had encountered obstacles from the beginning, and these soon proved insurmountable. Already in 1970 there had been several overtures to the General Synod from midwestern classes objecting to the new initiative, and in the face of these the board abandoned its intention to make it mandatory for all students in the RCA seminaries,[66] allowing continued admission to the seminaries separately. Also, there was difficulty with finances. At New Brunswick especially there were significant costs for accommodating an increased student body and a new faculty member, but no increased financial support from the churches, and, as Howard Hageman wrote later, "an institution which had paid its own way for many years was forced to draw out almost all of its capital reserves to meet its new expenses."[67] In addition, the presidency became a point of contention. Ridder resigned in 1971, and there were difficulties in replacing him, which reflected an ebbing of commitment on the church's part overall to the "unified" arrangement. With Lester Kuyper of Western Seminary serving as "interim president," in 1972 the BTE, by a slim majority, elected the denominational executive Arie Brouwer, the head of the General Program Council of the Reformed Church, as president, on the understanding that he would retain his position as director of the church's programs, thus presumably advancing the "unification" of the seminaries under denominational aegis. The BTE reported to the synod that year that the

29 Norman Thomas (1919-1999), class of 1944, dean 1969-1973;, provost 1973-1979; Herman Ridder (1925-2002), president 1969-1971; Virgil Rogers (1922-2005, faculty 1960-1986)

General Synod Executive Committee was pressing it to consolidate the seminaries at "one site," but there was resistance. "Obviously," observed the review committee on these matters, "such radical departures from the status quo have created tensions in the church." To add to everything else, enrollment in the program had declined from eighteen the first year to nine the second, and the prospective enrollment for the fall of 1972 was "uncertain."[68]

By 1973 it was evident in the BTE's report that the experiment with the new curriculum would be coming to a close. In the preceding year of 1972–73, after the unsuccessful attempt to appoint Brouwer, the board had dropped its commitment to a single presidency over both seminaries and a single budget for both schools. A new president for each school had been nominated—in New Brunswick's case, the Reformed Church pastor and scholar Howard Hageman, of whom we shall hear more. With the decision to return to separate budgets and separate presidents, the structure underneath the BLMS program was largely eroded. The board reported that it had attempted to "provide a rich, balanced flexible theological education meeting the demands of continuing programs, questioning almost every aspect of the theological enterprise as it now exists, making temporary decisions which would not compromise future creative action," but that it had proved problematic to create a "framework in which responsive and responsible decisions were and can continue to be made." And then in 1974 the board reported that though elements of the program would be "integrated" into the M.Div. curricula at each seminary, "no new students [will] be enrolled in the BLMS program as presently structured." So the experiment came to a close, and the last BLMS student was graduated in 1977.

The BLMS program has been remembered in very positive terms not only by students—of whom there were nineteen in all—who graduated from it,[69] but also by faculty who taught in it. And the years of experimentation were to have a continuing legacy. The Board of Theological Education would continue to serve until 1992 as an umbrella governing board that coordinated theological education in the church. In 1989 Paul Fries, who by then would be dean of New Brunswick Seminary, would lead the faculty in a major curricular revision that incorporated elements of the BLMS program, especially the groups for theological reflection and the concept of theological "motifs" as an organizing principle for courses.[70] But there would be no more serious talk of the "unification" of the two seminaries or their programs. Already as of late 1973, when Howard Hageman was installed as president, it was clear that New Brunswick Seminary would again be seeking out its mission as a discrete institution.

Postscript: Hiram Street

In late 1969, in expectation of an increased student enrollment at the start of the BLMS program the following year, the seminary acquired an abandoned hardware store on Hiram Street in downtown New Brunswick, intending to convert it into student housing. The choice of location reflected the values of the new curriculum: as Dean Thomas told the local newspaper, the project "provides additional student housing for an increased enrollment at NB, but it also indicates involvement in the city's problems and needs."[71] By the next spring, however, opposition to the plan emerged in the largely Puerto Rican neighborhood to what was seen as the seminary's intrusion. Seminary leaders found themselves needing to listen to the objections. Negotiations with neighborhood groups ensued, while the administration made other arrangements for the first wave of new students. Thomas wrote to a concerned local church member that "we have found in effect that the establishment of a comfortable residence for seminary students would hamper our ministry to the people living in the area," where low-cost housing was at a premium and people's reaction to what seemed to them a gentrification was "understandable."[72] As John W. Beardslee III put it, "We have learned what the real situation [is] in which our student must learn and participate."[73] By December, Thomas was ready to report a plan to the board that would incorporate more subsidized housing units than had originally been foreseen—a plan that, though he admitted its "financial feasibility" to be "on the margin," signified "real progress in establishing relationships with people in the community."[74] But later that month, and before the board had made any decision, a fire that was caused by arson severely damaged the building. The project came to a halt, and eventually the board sold the property.

αϖ

Although the Hiram Street project was brief and uncompleted, the attempt of the seminary's leaders to act on a "concern for the city's problems and needs," anticipated major themes in the school's life over the decades to come. This was true not only in their expression of a desire to reach beyond the bounds of the seminary and of the Reformed Church to serve the city that surrounded them, but in their glimpsed realization that if they were determined to make good on such a desire they would have to be willing to be changed themselves.

PART FOUR

A Commitment and Its Implications, 1973–2014

1 *The campus, ca. 1970*

In one sense, the state of New Brunswick Theological Seminary after the demise of the experiment of "unified" theological education in the Reformed Church was similar to its state before that program started: it had its own president, its own budget, and even though the Board of Theological Education (BTE) still existed, New Brunswick had a separate "Management Committee" within the BTE to consider its own affairs. But in another sense, a more profound sense, the seminary was permanently changed. Not only was the question of the viability of the school if it remained by itself—which had in part motivated the experiment and had been raised pointedly by consultants from the Association of Theological Schools in 1966, before the experiment began[1]—still pressing, but the denomination was busy posing its own questions about theological education and whether the existing seminaries were the best means to do it. In fact, as will be seen, the Reformed Church was soon to create another agency, beyond the seminaries, which offered a track for candidates to follow that would bypass the seminaries altogether, and, in that way, the connection to the denomination was on its way to becoming, if not less firm, at least less substantial. But most importantly, the spirit behind the experiment that was now past—the sense of urgency about theological education that is committed to engage with the world around it, especially the urban environment, a spirit that was larger than the experiment itself—remained at least as strong as when the experiment had been in place.

The commitment by the seminary to an engagement with its urban context was to be central to its history in the following forty years. This was a commitment that expanded its mission for the first time beyond its traditional task of supplying clergy for the Reformed Church in America, with wide-ranging consequences for all aspects of the seminary's life—student body, degree programs, curriculum, governance, faculty, and the campus itself.

The Vision of Howard Hageman

A graduate of the class of 1945, Howard G. Hageman had served for twenty-eight years as a pastor in downtown Newark, New Jersey, before returning to his alma mater as president. He brought many strengths to the task. He was well known throughout the Reformed Church, especially through a weekly column that he had contributed to its magazine, the *Church Herald*. He was also a respected scholar in the field of worship and liturgy, with a special affinity for the ideas of the nineteenth-century Mercersburg movement (of which, we recall, the seminary had once been a center of opposition), and in general stood for a Reformed spirituality centered upon the corporate, confessional, and liturgical aspects of the tradition. Also, as a long-term urban pastor, he had an acute sense of the needs of urban life and the responsibility of the church to respond to those needs, especially at the level of structures of economic and political power.[2]

In his inaugural address Hageman articulated a new vision for the school—in effect the first glimpse of what would develop as a long-term plan for its renewal—at a moment when, as he would later describe it, the seminary was suffering from compromised finances and low morale in the wake of the demise of the Bi-Level Multi-Site program and of the "unified" presidency.[3] His rhetoric was strikingly different from that of the framers of the BLMS experiment; he did not speak of levels of professional formation or of the pedagogy of group encounters or of fresh methods of approach to theological traditions. Indeed, he saw theological education in terms of a traditional dichotomy that those framers had specifically tried to avoid: he saw the seminary as basical-

A Commitment and Its Implications, 1973–2014

2 Howard G. Hageman (1921-1992), president, 1973-1985

3 Howard Hageman with student Robert Hoffman, 1976

ly maintaining a healthy tension between the academic and the practical, between being "a graduate school in religion" and being "a professional school for the training of…ministers." But if Hageman was stepping back from the school's recent innovations in *how* and *what* it would teach, he envisioned other innovations in the matter of *whom* it would teach.

In a word, Hageman envisioned a new community of *learners* at New Brunswick Seminary—a much more diverse community that it had ever been before. Speaking specifically from his experience as an urban pastor, he pointed to potential candidates for ministry among "minority" groups in Newark and by implication other cities. These people were needed as ministers in their churches but had neither the educational prerequisites nor the time for traditional study in a seminary; was there not a way for the seminary to help them? He also noted the lack of continuing education for those already in ministry who found aspects of their work "bewildering" and "frustrating," as well as the lack of theological education for lay people, not just clergy. And here he sketched out a vision that would bring seminary students

4   Five faculty members, ca. 1980: Paul Fries, Charles Wissink, Hugh Koops (1932-2001), John W. Beardslee III (1914-2001), Virgil Rogers (1922-2005)

together with these others for a theological education that would address them all and thus significantly widen the scope of the seminary's work. "Personally," he said, "I long to see the day when some classes at New Brunswick, probably held in the evening, involve seminary students, members of minority groups, ministers and lay people together in their composition. I think the mix would be rewarding for all of us." He admitted that he saw as yet no easy way to bring such a thing about, but was "convinced" that the "day has passed" when "we could think of theological education only as a cloistered experience" of young graduate students over a period of "detached years;" a seminary has in fact a "frighteningly large responsibility" not just for those students but "for the theological life and health of the whole church."[4]

Howard Hageman's inaugural vision would find remarkable fulfillment in the decades to follow. Classes "in the evening" became the wave of the future, and, though there would be no "mix" of students and non-students in quite the way he imagined, still, those classes would fill with people who otherwise lacked the opportunity for a theological education and significantly broaden the seminary's involvement with the "whole church."

An Opening: Evening Education

In the event, as Hageman had imagined, it was by means of an "evening program" that the seminary moved to broaden its base of students beyond the traditional limits of the Reformed Church and to engage with communities of color. Those moves had permanent results in the seminary's continuing commitments, as will be seen. Indeed, evening classes remain to this day the staple of its coursework—though the idea of an "evening program" as separate from a "day program" lasted only a little more than a decade and a half, from 1975 until the early 1990s.

It was in the spring of 1975 that Howard Hageman and his friend George (Bill) Webber, another veteran urban pastor who was then president of New York Theological Seminary (NYTS) in Manhattan, developed a plan for a partnership between their schools. NYTS did not then have the accreditation to allow it to offer the Master of Divinity degree but saw the potential for an evening degree program in New York City for part-time students. The two men's idea was that New Brunswick would supply the degree-granting authority for such a program, NYTS would supply the facilities, and the faculties of both institutions would together supply the instruction. Already that summer, New Brunswick was reporting to the General Synod its hopes that the collaboration—called at first simply the "Urban Program," and eventually "Graduate Education for Metropolitan Ministry" (GEMM)—would expand its ministry with black students.[5] As Webber described it in its first semester of operation, its aims were to reach, primarily, "Black and Hispanic clergy, presently engaged in ministry and duly ordained, but without previous seminary education," and, secondarily, young college-educated "leaders in Pentecostal and evangelical churches" and "older church leaders…who now seek educational credentials and perhaps ordination."[6] Already at its outset twenty students were enrolled, by the spring of 1977 there were thirty-one, and in 1982 there were thirty-five.[7] By the time the partnership ended in 1983, Benjamin Alicea, who had been the program's director since graduating from New Brunswick in 1978, counted

5   Benjamin Alicea and students, ca. 1980

twenty-five students who had earned the M.Div. degree through it.[8]

When the dissolution of the partnership with NYTS came, the faculty and administration at NBTS found it painful, but the dissolution resulted in part from the program's very success. Ostensibly, the NYTS faculty and administration withdrew from the program out of a feeling that New Brunswick, as the degree-granting institution, had assumed disproportionate authority over it. They also discovered that obstacles to receiving their own accreditation to grant degrees were considerably smaller than they had thought. There were also evident misunderstandings on both sides, born of the difficulties of maintaining the fine details of a partnership over a distance of miles (in which difficulties there were echoes of the experience of the "unified presidency" of Reformed Church seminaries a decade earlier). It was also true that these were different institutions in their style and character. New Brunswick was invested in a traditional Reformed curriculum, and, though its classical approach was arguably its gift and strength, NYTS had greater "flexibility," as Hageman had acknowledged in a letter to Webber,[9] and the difference led to frustrations on both sides. NYTS, at any rate, proceeded to develop the thriving evening program in Manhattan on its own.

Once it was clear that New York Theological Seminary was withdrawing from the partnership, the faculty and administration at New Brunswick moved immediately, in the spring of 1983, to plan their own evening program, with the same aims in mind as before. The seminary's report to the General Synod in 1983 already identified the First Reformed Church in Jamaica, Queens (thus not Manhattan), as the first site for the program; a year later, by which time the New York Board of Regents had approved the Queens program, the seminary had also decided to conduct evening classes at New Brunswick as well. Thus the program, known as the Evening Theological Education Program (ETEP), would have sites in two states, both within the broad New York metropolitan area.[10] In the spring of 1986, Robert White, who become president the previous year on Howard Hageman's retirement, reported his administration's satisfaction with the two-site arrangement as "workable and fruitful" and announced that enrollment during the spring semes-

6   Button promoting the Evening Theological Education Program, ca. 1986. worn by faculty and staff when visiting churches

7   Promotional materials for the Evening Program ca. 1985 featured the question "Who left the lights on at New Brunswick Seminary?"

ter—including evening enrollment—"set a new seminary record" at 147 students.[11]

It was also in 1986 that the seminary, having earlier negotiated a cooperative agreement with St. John's University in Queens, a Roman Catholic institution of the Vincentian Order, established St. John's as the New York site of the evening program.[12] The seminary maintained office space and had the use of classrooms at St. John's, and the students would take elective courses in the university's theology department that would count toward their New Brunswick degrees. The agreement has been remarkably resilient, remaining in place to the present.

A final note about the "evening program": it was sometime in the early 1990s that the faculty and administration ceased to think of the academic life of the seminary in terms of two separate programs defined by time of day. Students, indeed the majority of students, still took courses in the evening, and for the same reason that had brought the evening program into being in the first place: a great many were part-time students, who had jobs to attend to during the day. For its part, the school remained committed to offering all required courses in the evening, so that a student could complete a degree without attending at any other time. But the faculty taught the evening courses according to the same standards as the daytime courses. Moreover, any student was free to take courses any time of day, according to his or her own convenience. And so students were no longer designated as "day students" or "evening students";[13] James Seawood, who came to the seminary as "dean of evening students" in 1987, had become by 1995 simply the "dean of students."[14]

8 St. John Hall at St. John's University in Queens, site of the seminary's New York program

Sequels to Diversity

The seminary's embrace of evening education in 1975 inaugurated a period of momentous change in the composition of the student body and, eventually, of the faculty and staff as well. Up until the moment when the evening program opened, New Brunswick Seminary was, as it had been from the beginning, a school devoted almost exclusively to the preparation of ordained ministers for the Reformed Church in America. Accordingly, the whole seminary community—students, faculty, staff—was, like the denomination itself at the time, largely made up of white people, and the students were, as they had always been, mostly young and male. But after 1975 that community, beginning with the student body, contained an increasing proportion of people of color, and of women, to the point that both of those groups are now in the majority, and the average age of students has climbed into the forties.

9 Dean of students James Seawood (center, 1947-2014), with director of the St. John's program Richard Sturm (right) and John W. Beardslee III, ca. 1995

10 James Seawood with student Alma Mack, ca. 1992

The story of these remarkable changes over the past forty years is partly a matter of statistics. But it is also, more profoundly, a matter of *discourse*—of how the seminary has "talked about" the changes as they occurred, and accordingly how it has registered them and how they have altered its identity. That discourse has generally celebrated these changes themselves, but also, increasingly, it has addressed difficult questions of structural racism, power, and privilege.

In the 1970s, the impetus to reach a more diverse body of students came not just from the seminary's leadership, but also from the Reformed Church. At the tumultuous General Synod of 1969, during which the civil rights leader James Foreman confronted the church with the "Black Manifesto" of the National Black Economic Development Conference, calling white religious organizations to make reparation for their complicity in racism, the church had established an internal "Black Council" and pledged to "focus on race relations in urban work."[15] By 1975, in response to the synod's request for a report on "how the training of ethnic minority students could be implemented in our Seminaries," New Brunswick reported that it "has had extensive contact with the Black Council" and cited the developing plans for the collaboration with NYTS as a means to "expedite the training of black ministers."[16]

The process of diversification was halting at first. During the initial years of experience with the Evening Program, both during and after the period of collaboration with NYTS, seminary leaders, apparently considering the evening students as a separate group, did not tend to describe the overall student body as significantly diversified. Meanwhile the seminary made its first full-time appointments of persons of color to the faculty: Benjamin Alicea in 1978; Wilbur Washington, a Reformed Church minister and NBTS graduate who had been teaching at Central College in Iowa and who became in 1981 the first African American faculty member as assistant professor of homiletics and director of supervised ministry; and Marvin McMickle, associate professor of ministry. But Washington and McMickle were among the faculty members dismissed "with commendation and in good standing" in 1985 (McMickle remaining another year as an adjunct professor), when the administration of President White responded to a financial crisis by making deep budget cuts, and Alicea resigned in late 1986. The accreditation team of the Association of Theological Schools that visited the seminary that fall noted with concern McMickle's and Alicea's "impending departures," which would leave no people of color on the faculty.[17]

Soon, however, the inclusion of people of color became an official priority of the seminary. In his reports to the Board of Theological Education in 1986, White announced that there would be an intentional policy of "racial/ethnic representation in faculty and administrative appointments," to make the leadership of the seminary more diverse. Two years later the BTE took an action that two of the next four faculty appointments would be persons of color. (Eugene Sutton was appointed as faculty

11 *Students Jay Do Yu and Archie Richmond, ca. 1986*

member in preaching and worship in 1991, and Warren Dennis in urban ministry in 1992. Both are African American.)

12 *Warren Dennis at his Inauguration as Dirck Romeyn Professor of Metro-Urban Ministry in 2009*

13 Student Rufus McClendon, Jr. in the Great Hall of Sage Library, mid-1980s

White's reports also began routinely to break down the seminary enrollment by race and gender, and we can see how far the process of diversifying the student body had gone since 1975: in the fall of 1989 the student body comprised 73 Caucasians, 63 African Americans, 9 Asians, and 6 Hispanics, and among these there were 93 men and 58 women.[18] In 1992 the seminary reported to the General Synod, as a point of pride, that "African American students at NBTS comprise the highest enrollment percentage (45 percent) of any North American theological school, exclusive of the historic Black seminaries," and that "in 1991, for the first time, women students reached a slight majority in enrollment, while the number of older, part-time students continued to grow."[19]

It was also in 1991 that the seminary undertook an "Asian Initiative" to "open the doors of NBTS to the large number of Asian churches in the New York-New Jersey area and in the RCA."[20] It was a far-reaching program which included, among other things, continuing education for local Korean pastors, formal partnership agreements with seminaries in Korea, and Korean teaching assistants for Korean students in NBTS classes—all of which had the effect of encouraging Korean students to enroll at the seminary. These students have accounted for as much as 20 percent of the student body in subsequent years.

Under the presidency of Norman Kansfield, who succeeded Robert White in 1993, the diversity of the seminary community became a matter of particular celebration and a constant feature of the seminary's self-presentation. As Kansfield was later to note, in 1993 white students formed the majority of the student body, but by 1997 the proportions were 40 percent white, 40 percent African American and 20 percent Asian. This "distribution continued as almost automatic for several years"[21]—a situation in which no one group was in the majority—although by 2005 African Americans had begun to constitute a majority, as is still the case. In the Kansfield years, at any rate, the seminary's leadership emphasized the variety of traditions, denominations, and ethnicities as an asset to the educational program and as the expression of a fundamental Christian value. In his report to the General Synod in 1997, for instance, the president contrasted what the seminary "used to be," presumably before 1975, with the way it was then, in the late nineties. It had used to be "a very small family affair," but "God has been using the seminary in the larger Christian family, educating all as to what God's family is really about."[22]

A Commitment and Its Implications, 1973–2014

14 Korean Student Association (KOSAN) gathering, 2009. From left: Enu Ju Do, Jin-Pyoung Lim and child, Minkyung Hwang, family of Guncheol Kim, Ock kee Byun, Jiae Lee, affiliate professor Jinhong Kim, Guncheol Kim, Yongmin Lee, Mill Jeon, family of Yongmin Lee, Joel (Eun-yul) Kim, Wonhyo Titus Kim, Jin-Pyung Lim.

The nature of the seminary's discourse about its diversity then took a different and deepening turn, in 2005. In the spring of that year, around the time of President Kansfield's departure (on which, see below) when the moment seemed ripe for re-evaluation of the seminary's life at many levels, a group of students pressed the case to the Board of Trustees that for all the diversity of individuals at the school, the structures of power and the norms of interaction still privileged white people above others. In the phrase of James Cone, quoted by the student Gregory Dunlop at the time, there was "embedded racism" in the institution itself, which persisted beneath the evident variety of traditions and ethnicities represented in the seminary community, and a truly just diversity would not be possible until that racism was confronted.[23]

In response, the board committed the seminary to "address issues of race, power and privilege," and in the following year set in motion a process of anti-racist training and reflection, with the help of consultants, out of which an "Anti-Racist Transformation Team" was formed in 2007, with members from the faculty, administration, student body, and alumni/ae. This team has continued to examine the community and engage it in reflection on how to" "dismantle" institutional racism in all aspects of the seminary's life. The discussions about diversity therefore took on a new dimension, though diversity itself remained a core value; as President Gregg

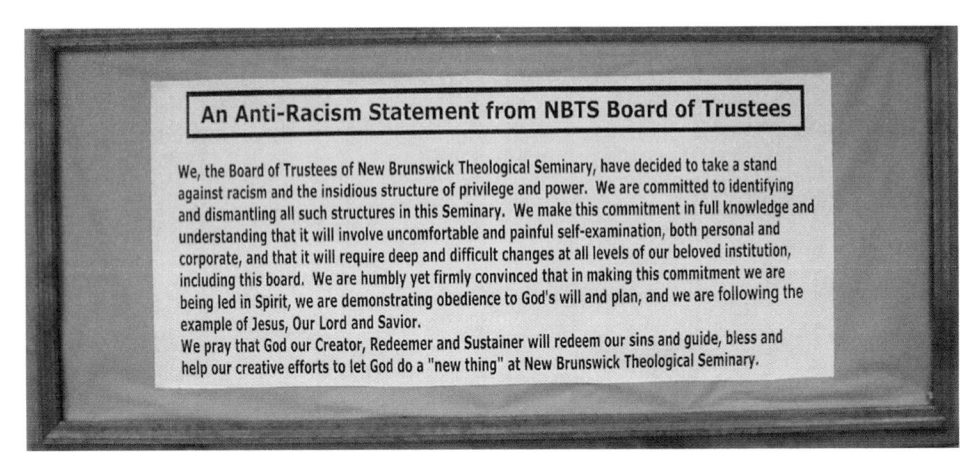

An Anti-Racism Statement from NBTS Board of Trustees

We, the Board of Trustees of New Brunswick Theological Seminary, have decided to take a stand against racism and the insidious structure of privilege and power. We are committed to identifying and dismantling all such structures in this Seminary. We make this commitment in full knowledge and understanding that it will involve uncomfortable and painful self-examination, both personal and corporate, and that it will require deep and difficult changes at all levels of our beloved institution, including this board. We are humbly yet firmly convinced that in making this commitment we are being led in Spirit, we are demonstrating obedience to God's will and plan, and we are following the example of Jesus, Our Lord and Savior.

We pray that God our Creator, Redeemer and Sustainer will redeem our sins and guide, bless and help our creative efforts to let God do a "new thing" at New Brunswick Theological Seminary.

15 Anti-racism poster mounted in the Hertzog Room in Zwemer Hall from ca. 2009 to 2014

Mast wrote in his report to the General Synod of 2008: "It has become essential to our faithfulness to the gospel and to the future of the seminary that [the seminary] is becoming a more passionate and articulate anti-racist and thus inclusive community of faith and learning."[24]

Meanwhile, diversity itself has proceeded apace; as of the present moment, a majority of the full-time faculty consists of people of color, and the dean of the seminary is African American: Willard Ashley, who joined the faculty in 2008 as director of supervised ministry and became dean in 2012.

The Presence of Women

The emerging diversity of the seminary community in the late decades of the twentieth century also included diversity of gender. This was the period in which women became a major presence in the student body and the faculty.

Proposals had been made as early as 1906 to admit female students. The superintendents' minutes for that year record an inquiry from a woman who was a college student at Stanford about "her possible admission here for preparation for the full and actual work of the ministry." The minutes lament that even though "our Church is sending out to her mission fields, many women of noble spirit and choice abilities who are…admitted to a voice in the control of all the affairs of the mission," still "we have no legislation on the part of General Synod concerning such cases,"[25] and thus the superintendents felt constrained not to open the doors of the school to women. It was not until 1961 that the first woman, Martha Houck, was admitted to take classes, apparently without being a degree candidate, and it was in 1971 that the school had its first female graduate, Margaret Yoder, who was later ordained in the Episcopal Church. The next women to graduate were L'Anni Hill-Alto and Klaire Miller in 1977, who were among the first women to be ordained in the Reformed Church in America, in 1978.

From 1977 onward, there was steady stream of female graduates, and women students quickly became a major presence in the school. By 1982, they accounted for 32 percent of the student body. In 1991 the

A Commitment and Its Implications, 1973–2014

16 Chapel scene in Zwemer Hall, ca. 1975

seminary reported to the General Synod that for the first time women formed a "slight majority," and since then the percentage has tended to be around the 50 percent mark or greater; in 2013 it was 55.3 percent.[26]

As for the presence of women in the faculty, although female missionaries frequently came to the seminary to give occasional lectures from the early 1900s onward, the first time that a woman was hired to give formal instruction appears to have been in 1939–40. This was when "Mrs. True Wager Mulder," co-taught the course in "Speech, Bible Reading, Sermon Delivery and Literary Interpretation."[27] Professor Bertha Paulsen, a distinguished Lutheran theologian from Gettysburg Seminary, taught a course at New Brunswick in pastoral counseling in 1950.[28] Several other women taught as ad-

17 Eileen Winter Esmark, class of 1978

18 Seminary graduates lining up outside Old Queen's for commencement at Kirkpatrick Chapel, ca. 1987

19 Elizabeth Johnson, professor of New Testament, preaching in the chapel in Zwemer Hall, late 1980s

juncts in the decades that followed. And Margaret Wilson served for twenty-nine years as librarian at Sage Library, most of that time as director of the library—a post that was, however, not yet a faculty position—before her retirement in 1957.[29] The first woman to serve as a full-time faculty member was Elizabeth Johnson, who served as professor of New Testament from 1986 to 1998. By 2013 women comprised 34 percent of the full-time faculty, and 43 percent of the part-time faculty.[30]

"The Reformed Church's Seminary," Revisited

It will be clear by now that the changes in the make-up of the seminary community after 1975 began with what was, in effect, a change in the mission of the school, even if it was not identified as such at first. Whereas traditionally the Reformed Church in America, and New Brunswick Seminary itself, had always understood its mission as the preparation of students for ministry within the denomination, in the wake of the experiment of the 1960s, the seminary began to conceive its mission as not just for the Reformed Church but for, as Howard Hageman put it, "the whole church," as it offered theological education that reached to Christian communities beyond the denomination's borders. The Reformed Church encouraged and supported New Brunswick Seminary in these changes, as we have seen. And yet the changes in the seminary's make-up, and in the communities it served, also meant that there would be changes in the school's relationship to the Reformed Church, which indeed has itself continued to consider new answers to the question, first broached in the 1920s, of how and whether its seminaries would best accomplish its task of theological education. The Reformed Church, in any event, no longer constituted the seminary's sole reason for being. And yet New Brunswick Seminary and the Reformed Church have continued to stand together in a close partnership, which has been evolving over these last forty years.

It has been the role of the seminary president, in particular, to take the lead in helping the institution articulate its mission. The idea that the school's mission was a mission *of* the Reformed Church in America—that is, on its *behalf*—and not simply *to* the Reformed Church in America, was implicit already in the words and actions of Howard Hageman. But it was Robert White, president from 1985 to 1992, who first stated this notion outright and explored the tensions inherent in it. In 1986, in a paper for the Board of Theological Education, he described New Brunswick Seminary as "an irreplaceable resource for theological education in the RCA and an ecumenical service to the larger church of Jesus Christ in the populous mid-Atlantic region," and he went on to reflect on the relationship between being "denominational" and being "ecumenical," setting the two descriptors in tension with each other. Giving a breakdown of the denominational make-up of the student body at that moment, in which RCA students numbered 45—35 percent of the total 130 students—he asked, on the one hand, how the seminary could retain its "Reformed identity and theology," i.e., its ancient identity rooted in the professorate of the Reformed Church in America, while becoming a self-evidently ecumenical community of learning; and, on the other hand, how it could be a genuinely ecumenical community of learning without giving to its "ecumenical constituencies," i.e., those other churches it serves, a place in its governance and leadership?[31] There was a tension here indeed, and, especially in formulating the second question, White was anticipating some of the concerns that came to the fore twenty years later and found expression in the antiracist analysis of the school's structures of authority.

By 1988 New Brunswick Seminary had adopted a mission statement that represented an attempt, not to resolve the "ecumenical/denominational" tension

20 Robert A. White, president 1985-1992

that White had described, but at least to acknowledge it, by framing the school's mission itself as an attempt to be both denominational and ecumenical. Thus, the seminary is "an institution of the RCA rooted in the reformed tradition and committed to providing leadership for the RCA," and is also an "ecumenical seminary...[dedicated] to serve men and women of all ages and racial/ethnic backgrounds...[and seeking] the integration of a classical theological education and the effective practice of minis-

21 Norman J. Kansfield, president 1993-2005

try in urban, suburban and village churches and institutions."[32] Under the administration of Norman Kansfield (1993–2005), the seminary adopted in 1997 another mission statement that is also structured around the denominational/ecumenical dichotomy, though with the implied tension less evident, as it describes New Brunswick Seminary as a "teaching institution of the RCA called by God to be a servant of the whole church of Jesus Christ."

Early in the administration of Gregg Mast (2006 to the present), the seminary discussed its mission yet again, but in different terms that no longer relied on the dichotomy of denominational/ecumenical. Mast himself, in his first report to the General Synod, described the seminary as "a denominational seminary with an ecumenical student body, committed to forming people for ministry in an interfaith world"—thus continuing to employ the "denominational/ecumenical" dichotomy (though also for the first time including interfaith relationships within the seminary's mission). But Mast reported a new mission statement to the General Synod in 2010, a statement that was adopted at the head of a new strategic plan:

22 Gregg A. Mast, president 2006-present

> Rooted in the Reformed tradition and centered in its trust in God's sovereignty and grace, the seminary is an intercultural, ecumenical school of Christian faith, learning and scholarship committed to metro-urban and global contexts.

This statement no longer *defines* New Brunswick as a seminary "of" the Reformed Church in America—and in that sense does not present it as a "denominational" seminary—but rather implies, as Mast went on to state in his own words to the synod, that the seminary would be a "faithful partner in mission *with* the Reformed Church in America as we care and inspire each other in God's amazing story of grace."[33] Thus the adjective "denominational" would no longer apply to the essence, as it were, of the seminary, but rather would designate one of its commitments.

Consistent with an emerging realization that its relationship with the Reformed Church was that of a partner, the seminary had meanwhile, in 1999, created a "Center for Reformed Church Studies," which was renamed the "Reformed Church Center" in 2007. The creation of this center rested on the assumption that the seminary community had become an ecumenical community, and that its relationship to the RCA would need to be cultivated intentionally, as *one* of the school's concerns. Thus, its purposes are (1) to encourage among RCA students within that community "a strong sense of belonging to the RCA," and (2) to offer to the denomination an opportunity and resources "to reflect critically and prophetically on the RCA's living traditions and its pressing concerns."[34]

The change in the relationship between the seminary and the Reformed Church in America was not one-sided, for the conviction grew as well in the Reformed Church, in the years that I am discussing here, that theological education could be properly an ecumenically shared enterprise. For the long term, the denomination's most significant move to reflect that conviction came in 1984, when it established a new agency that is called at the present moment the "Ministerial Formation Coordinating Agency (MFCA)." This agency has a function parallel to that of New Brunswick and Western seminaries: it supervises RCA students who are enrolled at non-RCA seminaries and provides a process to provide them the certificate—as had been originally the prerogative of the professorate, and by extension the two seminaries

23 The presentations at the Center's first conference were published as Concord Makes Strength: Essays in Reformed Ecumenism *(Grand Rapids: Eerdmans, 2002)*

of the denomination—for examination by their classes. This is a process that now routinely makes it possible for a wide variety of seminaries of other traditions to provide theological education for candidates within the Reformed Church in America, which therefore no longer has the same officially exclusive relationship with its historic seminaries as before.

If the overall relationship between the seminary and the Reformed Church has thus shifted in its terms over the last forty years, it is also true that the seminary's actual participation in the life of the denomination still stands in continuity with the past in many respects. The Reformed Church Center brings denominational leaders to the campus. The office of the "professor," now known as that of "General Synod professor," which was first held by Livingston, and until the 1960s was synonymous with a tenured appointment at the seminary, is still held by some faculty members who belong to the Reformed Church, and these and others are active in the church's affairs. And voices from New Brunswick, as in the past, sometimes have a controversial role in the denomination nationally, as in June of 2005 when Norman Kansfield, who until the spring of that year had been the seminary's president, was suspended for a time from ordained ministry by the General Synod for actions based on his convictions concerning a Christian approach to issues of homosexuality. The circumstances of that event were certainly particular to that moment, and the issues involved were particular to the present debates in American churches, rather than past debates. Still, the shape and tone of the controversy that surrounded it recalled the series of controversies involving New Brunswick figures such as Hugh Baillie MacLean, Edward Strong Worcester, and John De Witt, and the seminary's place in (as one might call it) the theological landscape

24 Dean Willard Ashley

of the Reformed Church seemed, at the time, familiar to many observers.

Programs: A Glimpse

In the period being discussed here, that is, in the last forty years, the seminary has instituted a number of new academic programs and curricular changes. This

25 Some faculty and administration in 1990: James Seawood, John Coakley, Elizabeth Johnson, Richard Weis, Norman Thomas, David Waanders, Renee House, Hugh Koops, Robert White, John Beardslee, Eugene Sutton

brief study of the school's long history is not the place to report them all. But an overview will illustrate the effects of the trends in constituency and mission that I have been discussing—and at some points also they suggest current resonances with earlier themes in the seminary's history.

The Master of Divinity degree program remains the centerpiece of the school's curriculum. It underwent major revision in 1989, when integrative courses were introduced as well as reflection groups on students' ministry experiences—all influenced by the Bi-Level Multi-

26 Certificate in Theological Studies graduation, 2014

site curriculum a decade and a half earlier and aimed at a closer connection between coursework and ministry experience. There was also a major expansion of the supervised ministry (field education) program. In 2000 the curriculum underwent another revision, adding a required course in public theology that was influenced by the new field of urban ministry represented by Warren Dennis, and also a required course in Christian spiritual disciplines. Another revision is planned for 2015, which will have a significant online element and will incorporate required coursework in antiracism.

The seminary also, in 1997, initiated a Doctor of Ministry program in the field of Metro-Urban Ministry, under Dennis's direction, which has been a pioneering effort in that field and has continued to the present. Two other D.Min. programs have recently begun: one in Congregational and Community Renewal, based in the Albany, New York, area, and one in Pastoral Care and Counseling, based at New Brunswick.

In 2005, the seminary initiated a two-year "Certificate in Theological Studies" program for students who may or may not have a bachelor's degree but who seek a more extensive theological education than they receive in their local churches. This program continues to the present, and a Spanish-language track was added in 2012. Classes are taught on Saturdays throughout the fall and spring semesters. This program resonates with Hageman's vision in 1975 of a seminary curriculum that would extend theological study beyond the community of degree-candidates. Among other new programs in the period have been several with an international focus. In 1974 Paul Fries, who was professor of systematic theology and had done his doctoral work at the University of Utrecht, organized an "International Summer School" in the Netherlands to give students (as well as alumni and other pastors and laypeople) an introduction to the Dutch traditions of theology and church life in which the seminary has historic roots; the program has continued to the present. It is scheduled biennially and has been directed in recent years by Allan Janssen, affiliate professor of theology. The seminary has also had several connections with South Africa. Before the end of apartheid, a series of Reformed pastors from the Black and Colored churches in that country came to New Brunswick to study, with financial help from the United Reformed Church in Somerville, New Jersey. More recently, Warren Dennis, professor of metro-urban ministry, has taken two groups of students on study trips to South Africa. Beth Tanner, professor of Old Testament, has recently taken a group of students on a sturdy trip to Israel and Palestine.

Connections with Korea have been particularly strong, especially since the establishment of the Asian Initiative in 1991, and have provided occasions for the seminary to recall and reflect on its history of involvement in world mission. The seminary has entered into formal partnerships with several Korean institutions, and, in honor of the missionary Horace Grant Underwood of the class of 1884 (see part 2 above), sponsored from 2002 to 2007 an annual Underwood Seminar at New Brunswick on the intersections of Korean and American Christianity. Since 2008 it has co-sponsored, with the Saemoonan Presbyterian Church of Seoul, an annual international

27 Eilia Tema with Robert White

Underwood Seminar that brings a major American or European theological scholar to Korea under the seminary's auspices. Recently, the seminary has established a Center for Global Christianity, directed by affiliate professor Jinhong Kim, with an emphasis on maintaining global relationships and partnerships.

Once Again, a New Campus

By 2009, it was becoming clear that the campus, which had been the seminary's glory when it was first built between 1855 and 1884, was no longer viable for the seminary's life and programs as these had evolved, and the Board of Trustees took a decisive step. It entered into negotiations, first directly with Rutgers University, and then with the New Brunswick Development Corporation (DEVCO), to sell more than half the campus for use by the university, with the intention of creating a new compact campus on the remaining land. Now, in 2014, that campus is in place. It consists of a large parking area and two buildings (as pictured on the cover of

28 A group of adjunct, affiliate and regular faculty at commencement, 2013. Front step: Richard Sturm, Bernadette Glover-Williams, Ray Du Bois. Second step: Renee House, Matilde Moros, Christopher Brennan, Raynard Smith, Beth Tanner. Back: Jaeseung Cha, Mark Taylor, Daniel Meeter, Gregg Mast, John Coakley, Jinhong Kim, Willard Ashley, David Waanders

this volume): the old Sage Library and the new structure at 35 Seminary Place, as yet unnamed, which includes a chapel, offices, and classrooms.

The path to the trustees' decision in 2009 had been a very long one, and for most of the way this endpoint had not been clear.

Finding adequate funding for the seminary had been a chronic problem since its very beginning, with the possible exception of those years when the efforts of Suydam, Sage, and Cornell provided the funds for the original campus. By the mid-twentieth century, the costs of maintaining that campus were becoming onerous. Capital fund drives underwrote some necessary repair and replacement of buildings: the United Synod Appeal in the 1960s which made possible the razing of Hertzog and Suydam halls and the construction of Scudder and Zwemer halls; the New Brunswick Commitment drive in 1981–84, which made possible an extensive renovation of the Wessels wing at Sage Library and the reorientation of the entrance of Zwemer Hall; and the Reformed Church's Putting People in Mission Drive, completed in 1990, which renovated the two old faculty residences on the east end of the campus, mostly for purposes of student housing. But, these extraordinary infusions of money notwithstanding, the maintenance not only of property but of program remained a constant worry, amid the ferment of new visions and initiatives. In 1987 President White, reporting to the Board of Theological Education on the "enthusiasm" and "affirmation" contained in the report of the accrediting team of the Association of Theological schools the previous fall, also noted the team's warning that the seminary remained "seriously under-funded."[35] Though deficits from year to year were often avoided, the underlying concern remained. As the president put it in a report to the seminary trustees in 1994, "Over the past decade New Brunswick Seminary has examined and reconfigured absolutely every aspect of its corporate self. We have the resources to do a genuinely outstanding job of preparing persons for ministry. *Except for money.*"[36]

A Commitment and Its Implications, 1973–2014

leased both of the former faculty residences on the east side of campus as well. Also, between 2003 and 2008 the seminary and the university, with other investing parties, made serious plans—which at first had been part of an ambitious plan for reconstructing the whole campus—to erect a large new apartment building on the campus, with a parking garage. These plans would have provided a revenue stream, but they stopped short of fruition.

The trustees' plan in 2009 to, as they put it, "monetize" a portion of the campus was not an entirely new idea, but it represented a quantum leap over previous moves in that direction. For, in return for a new building and an additional sum of money that would substantially increase the seminary's endowment, the plan called for the razing of every building on campus, except for Sage Library. It would represent the final abandonment of the nineteenth-century vision of the campus, which had in fact remained perceptible in the intervening years, even when some of the buildings had been replaced. More fundamentally, however, the decision was not merely a matter of financial expediency; it also grew

29 Apse of Sage Library before renovation, 1983-1984

Through the period we are discussing, a series of committees and task forces of the trustees and administration, under the leadership of President Gregg Mast, attempted to undertake long-term planning to find larger and steadier sources of income, with small success. The idea that the campus itself might be a source of income was not itself a new idea; as early as 1985, the seminary had leased one of the campus buildings (the house on Bishop Street that Profesor Raven had willed to the seminary) to the university, and as of 2007 the university

30 Dedication of Scholte reading court, Sage Library, 1984

31 Exterior of new building at night

32 Exterior of new chapel

33 Interior of new chapel

from the realization that the old campus was no longer a necessity for the seminary, especially as the result of its most recent evolution. Today the large majority of students commutes, and therefore there is less need for student housing (although there will be designated housing units available to students off-campus); it is no longer assumed that faculty will live on campus, as was once the case; and an upgrading of facilities for classrooms, offices, and the community life of students, such as the new building would provide, was overdue.

αϖ

After considerable discussion within the seminary and among its constituencies, a building committee was formed in 2012, which engaged an architect, Michael Farewell of Princeton. Several months of planning ensued. Ground was broken for the new building in July of 2013. It was ready for occupancy a year later, and, as I complete this narrative, plans are underway for its dedication in October of 2014. The new campus will acquire its own meanings for those who will occupy it, and it will help define the next phase of the seminary's history in ways which, of course, we cannot know. But like the old campus with its proud row of buildings, or indeed like the compact and dignified structure of Old Queen's, the expansive and accessible new building stands at least as a witness to the era of the seminary's life that produced it—and thus to all the struggles, hopes, and attempts of those to whom the seminary has been entrusted, in these recent decades, to be faithful to the task first given to John Henry Livingston two hundred and thirty years ago, nurturing and preparing men and women for the gospel ministry.

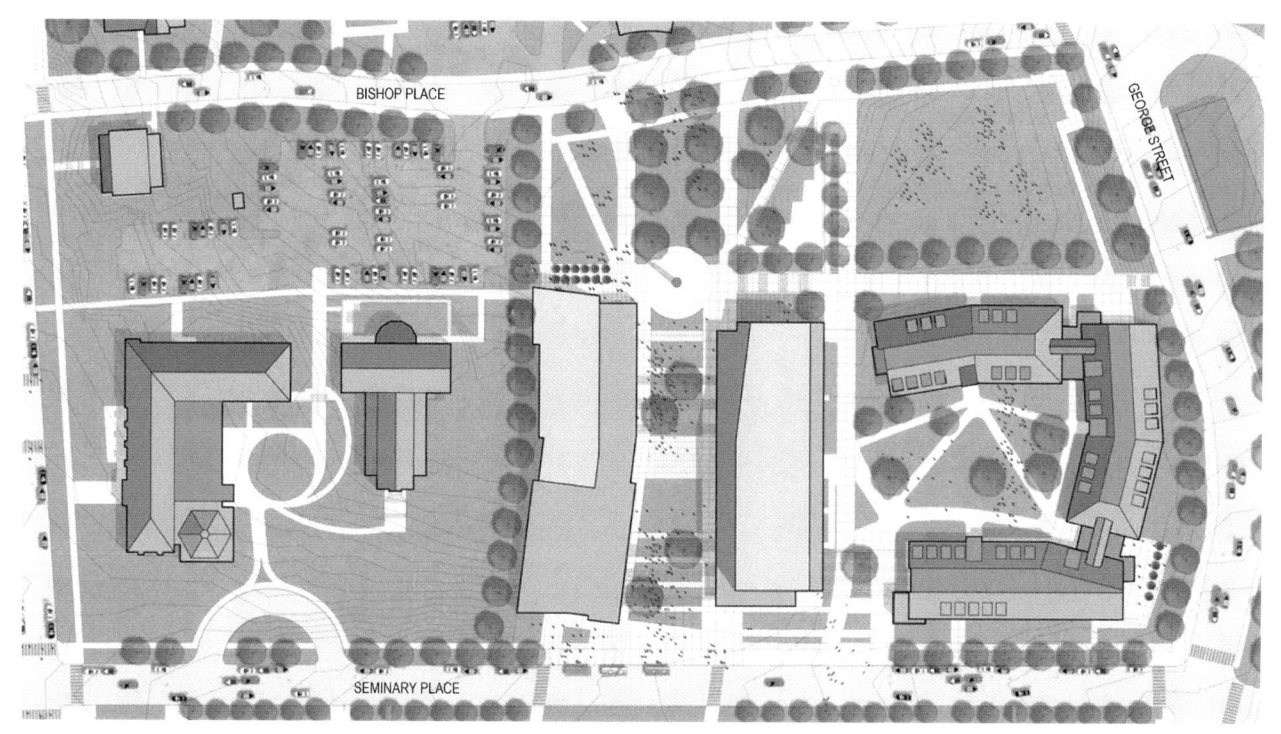

34 New seminary campus (left) with Rutgers campus (right)

Endnotes

Part One

1. *Ecclesiastical Records, State of New York*, vol. 6, ed. High Hastings (Albany: J.B. Lyon Company, 1906), 4122. The classis at this early juncture recommended settling Dutch professors within the Presbyterian college at Princeton, but this plan was never adopted.
2. *Acts and Proceedings of the General Synod of the Reformed Protestant Dutch Church in North America*, 1771–1812, 13–14 ("Articles of Union," arts. 28–29).
3. Robert W. Henderson, The *Teaching Office in the Reformed Tradition* (Philadelphia: Westminster, 1962), 156–94, 99–126.
4. John W. Coakley, "John Henry Livingston (1746-1825): Interpreter of the Dutch Reformed Tradition in the Early American Republic," in *Transatlantic Pieties: Dutch Clergy in Colonial American*, ed. Leon van den Broeke, Hans Krabbendam and Dirk Mouw (Grand Rapids: Eerdmans, 2012), 307-12.
5. *Charter of Queen's College* (New Brunswick: J. Terhune, 1850), 3.
6. Acts and Proceedings, 1807, 363.
7. Ibid., 365–66.
8. Alexander Gunn, *Memoirs of the Rev. John H. Livingston* (New York: Rutgers Press, 1829), 380–96.
9. John P. Wall, *Chronicles of New Brunswick, New Jersey* (New Brunswick: Thatcher-Anderson, 1931), 439.
10. A prospectus published at the time of the reopening of the college in 1825 (see below) describes the city as "healthful and pleasant" with good transportation and "facility of intercourse with the two great cities of New York and Philadelphia." Quoted by W.H.S. Demarest in *History of Rutgers College* (New Brunswick: Rutgers College, 1924), 288.
11. In the late 1820s, the seminary professors' quarters in the college were as follows: John De Witt in the east end and Selah Woodhull, and then James S. Cannon, in the west. "In the centre were the main class rooms where students of theology and college students alike met at their stated hours. On the second floor, east side, was the chapel, the room, later a drafting room and still later the fine arts room, which remained the chapel until the Kirkpatrick Chapel was completed in 1872. On the second floor, west side rear, was the library room, the room later given to history and political economy and later still to philosophy and psychology,

11 which remained the library until the Kirkpatrick Chapel, with its library accommodation, was completed," Demarest, *History of Rutgers College,* 287–88; also p. 310 for a description of the semirural setting of the college building as late as 1830.
12 There is an account of the building of Old Queen's in Demarest, *History of Rutgers College,* 20–23. On the residences of theological faculty, see E.T. Corwin, *Digest and Index of Synodical Legislation* (New York: Board of Publication of the RCA, 1906), 554–55.
13 David D. Demarest, "Some Memories Informally Written," typescript, NBTS Archives, 12-15.
14 Demarest, *History of Rutgers College,* 313, notes that "an advertisement in 1831 says that room with furniture and with board may be had for two dollars a week, and that cheaper rate may be found further from the city."
15 Thus Professor Milledoler in May 1832 alerted the superintendents to "a disposition manifested by the keepers of Boarding houses to raise the price of Board. Facilities offered in this respect by many surrounding Colleges and Theological Seminaries are such that unless prompt and efficient measures be taken to release our embarrassment, there is reason to apprehend that the number of our students instead of increasing must and will be diminished." Minutes of the Board of Superintendents, NBTS Archives (hereinafter BSM), 1:260; see also 1:59–60, 1:66, 1:264, 1:298, and 2:202.
16 U.S. Bureau of the Census. *Heads of Families at the First Census of the United States Taken in the Year 1790: New York.* (Washington: Government Printing Office, 1908), 134; *Population Schedules of the Second Census of the United States, 1800, New York,* reel 23 (Washington: National Archives Microfilm Publications), 270.
17 Philip Misevich, "In Pursuit of Human Cargo: Philip Livingston and the Voyage of the Sloop *Rhode Island*," *New York History* 86 (2005):185–204, esp. 189 n. 11.
18 L.A. Greene, "A History of Afro-Americans in New Jersey," *Journal of the Rutgers University Libraries* 56, no. 1 (1994): 11–20.
19 Demarest, "Some Memories," 2-3.
20 *Acts and Proceedings,* 1812, 430–33.
21 *The Constitution and Associate Statutes of the Theological Seminary in Andover; with a Sketch of Its Rise and Progress.* Published by Order of the Trustees (Boston: Farrand, Mallory, and Co, 1808), 19–20, 32–35.
22 The plan of a theological seminary adopted by the General Assembly of the Presbyterian Church in the United States of America, in their sessions of May last, A.D. 1811... (Philadelphia: Jane Aitken, 1811), 9–11.
23 Articles Explanatory of the Government and Discipline of the Reformed Dutch Church (1793), Art. XXII, in Corwin, *Digest and Index,* xxiv–xxvi.
24 The plan of a theological seminary..., 11–12.
25 The organization of the faculty is spoken of as early as 1827 (BSM 1:210), but it is not until 1838 that the faculty is supposed to have constituted itself and is directed to make a collective report (1:332); the first such report appears in 1840 (2:11).
26 E.g., BSM 1:280–88; the superintendents had occasion to remind the faculty of this principle in 1838, BSM 1:331.
27 BSM 1:244
28 BSM 1:184.
29 BSM 1:179.
30 Alexander McClelland, "Spiritual Regeneration Connected with the Use of Means," in J.W. Beardslee III, *Vision from the Hill* (Grand Rapids, Eerdmans, 1984), 47.
31 *Acts and Proceedings,* 1834, 317, 311.
32 Cannon, *Lectures on Pastoral Theology* (New York: Scribner, 1853), 585–601.
33 Gregg A. Mast, "A Decade of Hope and Despair: Mercersburg Theology's Impact on Two Reformed Denominations," in J. E. Nyenhuis, ed., *A Goodly Heritage: Essays in Honor of Elton J. Bruins* (Grand Rapids: Eerdmans, 2007), 163–80; Linden DeBie, "What Irked Dr. Berg?" *New Mercersburg Review* 30 (2002): 45–52.
34 *Acts and Proceedings,* 1860, 559.
35 Corwin, *Digest,* 704–09, indexes and summarizes the long string of synodical actions on the issue.
36 *Acts and Proceedings,* 1860, 559.
37 BSM 2:17–22.
38 *Acts and Proceedings,* 1841, 12–13.
39 *Acts and Proceedings,* 1841, 24.
40 *Acts and Proceedings,* 1841, 11.

41 BSM 1:336. Italics mine.
42 Luman Shafer, *History of the Society of Inquiry, 1811–1911* (New Brunswick: Laidlie Fund, 1912), 7–9.
43 Minutes of the Society of Inquiry, NBTS Archives (hereinafter SIM), 1:8. Such debates appear to have been discontinued after 1842; however, in 1853 they were briefly revived, but the question in May of that year—"is the present mode of conducting Missions the best that could be devised?"—appears to have been offensive to Jared Scudder (see part 2), whose family was deeply involved in the "present mode of conducting missions," and another debate was instigated, this time about whether to have debates—resulting in a vote of the society in the negative (SIM 1:137). Debates however did continue to appear, sporadically, in the later minutes.
44 G.R. Williamson, *Memoir of the Rev. David Abeel, D.D., Late Missionary to China* (New York: Robert Carter, 1848); Alvin J. Poppen, "The Life and Work of David Abeel" (S.T.M. thesis, Union Theological Seminary, n.d.).
45 *Acts and Proceedings*, 1852, 183. Gerald De Jong, *Mission to Borneo* (New Brunswick, NJ: Historical Society, RCA, 1989) provides a narrative history of the mission.
46 E.T. Corwin, *Manual of the Reformed Church in America*, 4th ed. (New York: Board of Publications, 1902), 770.
47 Demarest, *History of Rutgers College*, 217.
48 *Acts and Proceedings*, 1822, 23.
49 *Acts and Proceedings*, 1825, 35.
50 *Acts and Proceedings*, 1825 (Sept.), 20–24.
51 Demarest, *History of Rutgers College*, 327.
52 *Acts and Proceedings*, 1832, 137.
53 *Acts and Proceedings*, 1836, 515.
54 *Acts and Proceedings*, 1838, 173–74.
55 *Acts and Proceedings*, 1839, 306–07.
56 *Acts and Proceedings*, 1840, 395, 404–05.
57 *Acts and Proceedings*, 1850, 85–89.

Part Two

1 BSM 2:202–03; Demarest, *History of Rutgers College*, 381; *Acts and Proceedings*, 1855, 591.
2 *Acts and Proceedings*, 1856, 38.
3 *Acts and Proceedings*, 1857, 202, 210.
4 *Acts and Proceedings*, 1859, 439.
5 BSM 2:328–29.
6 BSM 2:380.
7 *Acts and Proceedings*, 1864, 462.
8 *Acts and Proceedings*, 1867, 264–65, 267–70.
9 Corwin, *Manual*, 4th ed., 392.
10 Corwin, *Digest of Synodical Legislation*, s.v. "Professorial Residences," 554–55; D. Demarest, "Historical Discourse," in David D. Demarest, Paul D. Van Cleef, and Edward T. Corwin, eds., *Centennial of the Theological Seminary, of the Reformed Church in America* (New Brunswick, NJ: Theological Seminary of the Reformed Church in America, 1884), 134–40.
11 *Centennial of the Theological Seminary*, facing p. 49. This was not a new image when it appeared in the volume, but rather a slightly revised version of an engraving that had appeared in print as early as thirteen years previously, as the frontispiece to the published proceedings of the inauguration of Professor Van Zandt (*Inauguration of the Rev. A.B. Van Zandt, D. D….* (New York: Board of Publication of the RCA, 1872). Remarkably, the image even at that earlier date included the fifth professorial residence as well as Sage Library, which was not built until three years later and to which, in that imagined rendering, the artist gave a pillared portico to match that of Suydam Hall (corrected in the centennial version to represent the actual appearance of the building which by then had been constructed). Clearly the prospect in all its grandeur had been long planned.
12 BSM 2:436.
13 *Acts and Proceedings*, 1868, 477.
14 Ibid.
15 *Annual Report of the Standing Committee on the Peter Hertzog Theological Hall to the Board of Superintendents of the Theological Seminary, Submitted May 18, 1870* (New York: Board of Publication of the RCA, 1870), 3, 4–11.
16 Corwin, *Manual*, 4th ed., 866. "The acknowledged ability, learning, and weight of character which distinguish the Professor elect, the tried and faithful services of the learned

and able men with whom he is to be associated, and the hope clearly held out to the Synod of the endowment of an additional Professorship, promise to give to Hertzog Hall such eminence before our own and other Churches as it has never yet enjoyed." *Acts and Proceedings*, 1871, 515.
17. *Acts and Proceedings*, 1871, 512–13.
18. BSM 3:211–12.
19. *Nineteenth Annual Report of the Standing Committee on the Seminary Grounds and Property...* (New York: Board of Publication of the RCA, 1888), 4.
20. BSM 3:771.
21. BSM 3:572.
22. *Sixth Annual Report of the Standing Committee on the Peter Hertzog Theological Hall...* (New York: Board of Publications of the RCA, 1875), 8.
23. Ibid., 11–15.
24. BSM 3:338.
25. *Sixth Annual Report*, 14–15.
26. E.g., *Acts and Proceedings*, 1879, 388–89.
27. *Acts and Proceedings*, 1911, 75–76.
28. Corwin, *Digest*, 778–79; Standing Committee Report 1888, 6 (on the portraits); Peter Wild, *John C. Van Dyke: An Essay and a Bibliography* (Tucson: Univ. of Arizona Library, 2001).
29. Dennis Voskuil, "When East Meets West: Theological Education and the Unity of the Reformed Church in America," in James Brumm, ed., *Tools for Understanding: Essays in Honor of Donald J. Bruggink* (Grand Rapids: Eerdmans, 2008), 201–30.
30. BSM 2:423 (May 1867).
31. Dirk Broek, quoted in Voskuil, "When East Meets West," 213.
32. John De Witt, *What Is Inspiration?* (New York: Anson D.F. Randolph, 1893), 3.
33. Egbert Winter, *What Is Inspiration?* (Grand Rapids: privately printed, 1894).
34. BSM, vol. 3, 77–78.
35. The historian Noel Erskine has pointed out that in 1902 and 1904, the annual reports of the RCA Board of Domestic Missions refer to William L. Johnson, who had been licensed and ordained by the classis of New York in 1869–1870, as having graduated from New Brunswick (Erskine, *Black People and the Reformed Church in America* [New York: Reformed Church Press, 1978], 63.) Johnson's name, however, does not appear in seminary records, and in granting him a dispensation for ordination, the General Synod of 1869 described Johnson as "a graduate of Lincoln University, Oxford, Pennsylvania" where he had "pursued a full collegiate and theological course." *Acts and Proceedings*, 1869, 622. See also John W. Beardslee III, "The Reformed Church in America and the African American Community," *Reformed Review* 46 (1992), 108.
36. Corwin, *Manual* (1902), 314–15, 891.
37. *Christian Intelligencer*, Nov. 11, 1880, 9 (memorial of Walden by Joseph E. Roy of the American Missionary Association).
38. Corwin, *Manual*, 314–15.
39. Islay Walden, *Walden's Miscellaneous Poems, Which The Author Desires to Dedicate to the Cause of Education and Humanity* (Washington: Reed and Woodward, 1872), and *Walden's Sacred Poems, with a Sketch of His Life* (New Brunswick: Terhune & Van Anglen, 1877).
40. Islay Walden to David Demarest, Sept. 21, 1878, Archives of the RCA.
41. Demarest, "Historical Discourse," in *Centennial of the Theological Seminary*, 116.
42. Samuel Zwemer made such a survey in 1934: "The Contribution of the Seminary to Foreign Missions," in W.H.S. Demarest, ed., *The One Hundred Fiftieth Anniversary of the Founding of New Brunswick Theological Seminary* (New Brunswick: privately printed, 1934), 37–50.
43. Norman Goodall, *Christian Ambassador: A Life of A. Livingston Warnshuis* (Manhasset, N.Y.: Channel Press, 1963).
44. Jacob Chamberlain, *In the Tiger Jungle and Other Stories of Missionary Work among the Telugus of India* (New York: Revell, 1896); *The Cobra's Den, and Other Stories of Missionary Work among the Telugus of India* (New York: Revell, 1900); *The Kingdom in India, Its Progress and Its Promise, with a Biographical Sketch by Henry Nitchie Cobb* (New York: Revell, 1908).
45. The standard account in English is still Lilias Underwood, *Underwood of Korea* (New York: Revell, 1918).
46. Samuel Zwemer and James Cantine, *The Golden Milestone: Reminiscences of Pioneer Days Fifty Years Ago in Arabia* (New York: Revell, 1938), 18.

47 Zwemer and Cantine, *Golden Milestone*; Alfred D. Mason and Frederick J. Barny, *History of the Arabian Mission* (New York: Board of Foreign Missions of the RCA, 1926); Lewis R. Scudder III, *The Arabian Mission's Story: In Search of Abraham's Other Son* (Grand Rapids: Eerdmans, 1998).

48 "Has the Dutch Church in choosing Borneo, Java, &c. as their missionary field, selected the best field of labor?" (March 1841); "Should the Dutch Church distinguish herself as the Missionary church of America" (March 1860).

49 Anon., "The Interseminary Movement," *Christian Education*, vol. 19, no. 3 (Feb. 1936), 231; Luman Shafer, *History of the Society of Inquiry* (New Brunswick: Laidlie Fund, 1912), 36–37.

50 The lectureship was revived at least once in later years. See *Acts and Proceedings*, 1964.

51 Walter Rauschenbusch. *A Theology for the Social Gospel* (New York: Macmillan, 1917), 1–22.

52 Schenck, *The Ten Commandments and the Lord's Prayer: A Sociological Study* (New York and London: Funk & Wagnalls, 1902), 111. On Schenck, see Lynn Japinga, "Responsible for Righteousness: Social Thought and Action in the Reformed Church in America, 1901–1941" (Ph.D. diss., Union Theological Seminary, 1992).

53 Quoted in Louise C. Wade, *Graham Taylor: Pioneer for Social Justice, 1851–1938* (Chicago: Univ. of Chicago Press, 1964), 44.

54 Jo Ann O. Robinson, *Abraham Went Out: A Biography of A.J. Muste* (Philadelphia: Temple Univ. Press, 1981).

55 *Acts and Proceedings*, 1883, 221–22.

56 *Acts and Proceedings*, 1898, 93.

57 *Acts and Proceedings*, 1916, 725. See part 3 on the question of what field the sixth professorship would cover, a question debated well into the 1920s.

58 *Acts and Proceedings*, 1906, 437.

59 *Acts and Proceedings*, 1894, 79.

60 *Acts and Proceedings*, 1920, 83.

Part Three

1 *Acts and Proceedings*, 1922, 780.
2 *Acts and Proceedings*, 1924, 96.
3 Hill, "What About Our Seminaries?" *Christian Intelligencer and Mission Field* [hereinafter *CI&MF*], Feb. 21, 1923, 114–15; William Louis Sahler, class of 1904, made the point more sharply later in the discussion: "Is it now worth while trying to keep alive a dwindling institution, when 16 miles away there is a growing one, which can train the men just as well, if not better, at not more than half the expense to our churches?" Sahler, "How Shall We Face the Seminary Crisis?" May 2, 1924, 274–75.
4 French, "What About Our Seminaries?" *CI&MF*, April 4, 1923, 210–11. An introductory note by the editor registers alarm at French's announcement of the defections, which "reveals that conditions in our beloved institution are critical," ibid., 209.
5 There was pushback on this point: E. J. Blekkink, a New Brunswick graduate of 1886 who had become professor of systematic theology at Western Seminary, declared theology, "the knowledge of God as revealed by Jesus Christ in nature and revelation and authoritatively embodied in the Scriptures," to be the great, indeed all-encompassing, subject of the seminary curriculum. Blekkink, "What Shall We Teach in Our Seminaries?" *CI&MF*, March 7, 1924, 147–48.
6 J.F. Berg, "A Seminary Curriculum for the Modern Minister," *CI&MF*, Nov. 1, 1923, 694–95.
7 J.H. Gillespie, "Church and Seminary," *CI&MF*, May 2, 1924, 276–77.
8 *Acts and Proceedings*, 1924, 104–05.
9 BSM 5:60–61.
10 Hageman traces the changes in the policy over that period in *Two Centuries Plus*, 111–12, 121, 138–39, 142.
11 BSM 5: 52, 134; the seminary also had applied for and received accreditation from the New York Board of Regents in 1929; ibid, 79.
12 BSM 5:52.
13 BSM 5:63, 87.
14 The address was 9 and 11 Seminary Place. BMM, 306.
15 Minutes of the Board of Directors (hereinafter, BDM) 56, 84.
16 BDM, 306.
17 *Acts and Proceedings,* 1934, 637.

Endnotes, pages 61-76

18. BSM 5:134.
19. "Dr. Demarest's Speech at General Synod in 1923 Nominating Dr. Worcester professor of Systematic Theology," (typescript), Worcester file, Archives of the RCA.
20. Untitled typescript beginning "I. How much weight is to be attached...," Worcester file, Archives of the RCA.
21. Untitled broadside beginning "DEAR BROTHER:--" [addressed to synod delegates], Worcester file, Archives of the RCA.
22. Hageman, *Two Centuries Plus*, 134.
23. Hospers to Demarest, June 25, 1923, 2. Worcester file, Archives of the RCA.
24. Frances Beardslee to John W. Beardslee, Jr., June 13, 1923.
25. Theodore Bayles, untitled address, in *Inauguration of Theodore Floyd Bayles...* (New Brunswick: Archibald Laidlie, D.D., Memorial Fund, 1925), 40.
26. Milton Hoffman, "The Living Past," in *Inauguration of Rev. Milton J. Hoffman...*, 41, 51.
27. William Weber, "How Shall the Church Speak to the New Age out of Eternity?" in *The Inauguration of Rev. William A. Weber...* (New Brunswick: Archibald Laidlie, D.D., Memorial Fund, 1926), 62.
28. John H. Raven, [Reminiscence of E.S. Worcester], *New Brunswick Seminary Bulletin* 11, no. 3 (Oct. 1937):3.
29. *Acts and Proceedings*, 1937, 75.
30. BSM 5:148, 156.
31. BSM 6:7
32. BSM 5:164–65 and 6:8, 26 (Muste); 5:86 (Buttrick); 5:156 (Peale).
33. BSM 6:59.
34. BSM 6:192.
35. BDM, 203, 225, 236.
36. *Acts and Proceedings*, 1959, 34.
37. Mary Kansfield, "Leave It to the Ladies," unpublished paper (presented at the 50th Anniversary Celebration of the... Women's Auxiliary, October 19, 2002), NBTS Archives.
38. *Acts and Proceedings*, 1957, 39.
39. MacLean, *Inaugural Address...The Relevance of the Old Testament* (New Brunswick: Privately printed, 1948), 7. The lecture was reprinted in the *Church Herald*, Oct. 22, 1948, 16–17, 22, and later in Beardslee, *Vision from the Hill*, 138–50.
40. *Acts and Proceedings*, 1949, 69–73.
41. BSM 6:60–61.
42. As examples of this generally neo-orthodox disposition, see the inaugural lectures of Justin Vander Kolk as Suydam Professor of Systematic Theology ("The Theologian's Task," in *Addresses on the Occasion of the Installation of the Reverend Justin Vander Kolk...* [New Brunswick, privately printed, 1951], 1–3); Vernon Kooy as De Witt Professor of Hellenistic Greek and New Testament Exegesis ("The Revelation of God in Jesus Christ," in *New Brunswick Theological Seminary Bulletin*, Feb. 1956, 2–8) (even though cautious and conservative in embracing historical criticism); and Virgil Rogers as Sage Professor of Old Testament Languages and Exegesis ("Toward an Understanding of Biblical Scholarship," in *Addresses on the Occasion of the Installation of the Reverend Virgil M. Rogers...* [New Brunswick: Laidlie Memorial Fund, 1962], 7–14).
43. See William R. Hutchison, *Errand into the World: American Protestant Thought and Foreign Missions* (Chicago: Univ. of Chicago Press, 1993), esp. 125–75.
44. BDM, 217.
45. BDM, 230–31.
46. BDM,. 235.
47. *Acts and Proceedings*, 1961, 43.
48. BDM, 257, 268–69, 284.
49. Hageman, *Two Centuries Plus,* 175.
50. BDM, 314–15.
51. BSM 6:[unnumbered] (meeting of Oct. 7–8, 1964).
52. BDM, 317.
53. BDM, 317; BSM, 287; *Acts and Proceedings,* 1964, 49.
54. Jamison, "Position Paper No. 1: The Purpose of Theological Education in the Reformed Church," in "Jamison—Permanent Committee 1963–65" papers, NBTS Archives.
55. *Acts and Proceedings*, 1965, 45.
56. BSM, 6:298–99.
57. BDM, 326.
58. BSM 6:1–3 (second paginaton).
59. *Acts and Proceedings*, 1966, 44–50, 165.
60. BSM 6:4–5 (second pagination).
61. *Acts and Proceedings*, 1969, 42.
62. "Theological Curriculum for the 1970s," *Theological Education* 4 (1968): 671–727. Though not cited, the concepts

of ministry as profession and theological education as professional education as articulated by Kaufman's teacher H. Richard Niebuhr in *The Purpose of the Church and Its Ministry* (New York: Harper, 1956) lay in the background of the ATS plan.
63 Program Design Committee to faculty members [of the two seminaries], memorandum, July 30, 1968, "Merger 1966–69" papers, NBTS Archives; *Acts and Proceedings*, 1969, 36–38.
64 Report of New Brunswick faculty June 25, 1970, on planning for Level One. "Bilevel Multisite" folder, NBTS Archives.
65 *Acts and Proceedings*, 1971, 27.
66 Hageman, *Two Centuries Plus*, 184.
67 Ibid., 188.
68 *Acts and Proceedings*, 1972, 31, 27.
69 Norman Kansfield, "The President's Role in Theological Education," in George Brown, Jr., ed., *Herman J. Ridder: Contextual Preacher and President*, 21–52 (Grand Rapids: Eerdmans, 2008), 48.
70 "Curriculum for a Third Century," NBTS Archives.
71 "Planners OK Hiram Street Apartments," *Home News*, Nov. 11, 1969.
72 Norman Thomas to Robert Shipman, April 24, 1970. Hiram Street papers, NBTS Archives.
73 John W. Beardslee to Herman Ridder, Dec. 2, 1970. Hiram Street papers, NBTS Archives.
74 Norman Thomas to Herman Ridder, Dec. 3, 1970. Hiram Street papers, NBTS Archives.

Part Four

1 "Report of [ATS consultants] C.L. Taylor and H.N. Morse to the New Brunswick Theological Seminary," Jan. 13, 1966. "Merger 1966–69" papers, NBTS Archives.
2 On Hageman, see Gregg Mast, *In Remembrance and Hope: The Ministry and Vision of Howard G. Hageman*, (Grand Rapids: Eerdmans, 1998).
3 Hageman, *Two Centuries Plus*, 187.
4 Hageman, inaugural address, typescript, NBTS Archives.
5 *Acts and Proceedings*, 1975, 31.
6 George Webber to Howard Hageman, Nov. 25, 1975. NYTS collaboration papers, NBTS Archives.
7 *Acts and Proceedings*, 1975, 158; 1982, 192.
8 Alicea, Report to the New Brunswick faculty and Management Committee on GEMM, March 4, 1983.
9 Howard Hageman to George Webber, Oct. 17, 1980. NYTS collaboration papers, NBTS Archives.
10 *Acts and Proceedings*, 1983, 223; 1984, 199.
11 NBTS President's Report, p. 3, in Board of Theological Education Minutes (hereinafter BTEM), 1986; *Acts and Proceedings*, 1986, 223.
12 BTEM, Apr. 1986, 4.
13 The campus telephone directory in the spring of 1993 designates students at the New Brunswick campus as either "Day" or "Evening"; in the fall directory of that year these designations have disappeared.
14 Dean of Student's Report, Board of Trustees Minutes (hereinafter BTM), June, 1995.
15 *Acts and Proceedings*, 1969, 98–99.
16 *Acts and Proceedings*, 1974, 39; 1975, 31.
17 ATS visitation report, 2, in BTEM, Apr., 1987.
18 BTEM, Apr. 1989, 2.
19 *Acts and Proceedings*, 1992, 315.
20 *Acts and Proceedings*, 1992, 316.
21 BTM, Apr. 2005, 2.
22 *Acts and Proceedings*, 2005, 297–98.
23 Gregory Dunlop, "Multi-Cultural Ministry: Responding to the Great Commission," paper presented to the Board of Trustees (Apr. 2005), 4.
24 *Acts and Proceedings*, 2008, 288.
25 BSM 5:610–11.
26 *Acts and Proceedings*, 1992, 315; NBTS 2014 self-study for the Association of Theological Schools, 6.
27 BSM 5:185.
28 BSM 6:123.
29 BSM 6:190.
30 2014 self-study, 54.
31 "Points of Tension, Possibilities for Growth, in RCA Preparation for Ministry," paper appended to BTEM, Apr. 1986, 1–2, 7, 4.
32 *Acts and Proceedings*, 1988, 250.

33 *Acts and Proceedings,* 2010, 488. Italics mine.
34 Mission statement of the Reformed Church Center, BTM, Jan. 2007.
35 BTE Minutes, Apr. 1987, 2.

36 BTM, Oct. 1994, President's Report, 1. Italics mine.

Sources for images
All images are courtesy of the Archives of the Reformed Church in America, Gardner A. Sage Library, and the New Brunswick Theological Seminary, except:

I.1	New York Historical Society
I.3	Collegiate Church Archives, New York
I.8	From: Barber, John W., and Henry Howe, *Historical Collections of the State of New Jersey* (New York: S. Tuttle, 1846), facing p. 312.
I.9	Rutgers University Archives
I.11	Rutgers University Special Collections
I.12	New Brunswick Public Library
I.13	West End Collegiate Church
II.2b	Rutgers University Archives
II.4	Rutgers University Archives
II.5	Rutgers University Archives
II.29	Archives of the Saemoonan Presbyterian Church, Seoul.
III.1	Rutgers University Archives
IV.34	New Brunswick Development Corporation (DEVCO)

Index

Abeel, David, *19*, 20
Adam (biblical figure), 63–64
African Americans: in New Brunswick, 10–11; in New Brunswick Seminary, 43–44, *70*, 91–92, 94
Albany, First [Reformed] Church in, 13, 67, 76
Alicea, Benjamin, 87, *87*, 91
American Bible Society, 46
American Standard Version translation committee, table of, 39
Amoy Mission, 21, *22*, 45–46
Andover Theological Seminary, 11
anti–racism, 93–94, *94*
Anti–Racist Transformation Team (ARTT), 93
Arabian Mission, 48, 70
Arabian Mission Hymn, *49*
Arcot Mission, 46
Arminianism, 64
Ashley, Willard, 94, *100*, *104*
Asian Initiative, 92
Association of Theological Schools (ATS), 66, 76–80, 84, 91, 104

Athens, NY, Reformed Church in, 20
Ayler, Junius G., 44

Bachelor of Divinity degree, 59–60, 77
Badeau, John S., 70
Bast, Henry, 69
Bayles, Theodore F., 60, *60*, 65
Beardslee, Frances, *66*, 67, 114 n.24
Beardslee, John W., Sr., *61*
Beardslee, John W., Jr., *60*, *61*, 65–66, *66*
Beardslee, John W. III, 80, *90*, *101*, 86
Belgic Confession, 63
Berean Society, 19
Berg, J. Frederic, 57, *57*, 64
Berg, Joseph Frederick, 16, 32, 37
Bergen, John H., 43–44, *44*
Bi-Level Multi-Site Program, 76–80
Black Manifesto, 90
Blekkink, E.J., 113 n.5
Board of Directors of New Brunswick Theological Seminary: established, 58; name changed from Board of Managers, 58

117

Board of Superintendents of New Brunswick Theological Seminary: as nominators of professors, 52; established, 5; examination of students by, 12–13, 16, 18, 66; opposition to student preaching, 16–17; powers of, 11; recognition of seminary's role in foreign mission, 19; reorganization of, 37; role of in early nineteenth century, 12–14; W.H.S. Demarest as member of, 59

Board of Theological Education, 75–76, 80, 84

Borneo Mission, 20–21, *21*

Brennan, Christopher, *104*

Brouwer, Arie, 79

Burrell, James, 57

Byun, Ock–kee, 93

Campbell, William H., 28, *28*

campus: construction of, 39–35; *29, 31, 34, 35, 61*; demolition of, 105; engraving of, 35, 111 n.11; map of, *62*; move to, from Old Queen's, 28–29; new building constructed in, 105, *106*, plans for, 71–75; replacement of buildings in, 67; sale of portion of, 105–106, *107*

Cannon, James Spencer, 14–16, *16*

Canons of Dort, 63–64

Cantine, James, 48, *48*

Center for Global Christianity, 103

Center for Reformed Church Studies. *See* Reformed Church Center

Certificate, Professorial, 3, *3*, 59

Certificate in Theological Studies program, 102, *102*

Cha, Jaeseung, *104*

Chairs, faculty. *See* Professorships

Chamberlain, Jacob, 46, *47*

Chamberlain, Lewis, 46

Chamberlain, William, 46

Chambers, Talbot W., 39, *39*

Chicago Commons, 50

Chicago Theological Seminary, 50

China, mission to. *See* Amoy Mission

Chosun Christian College (Seoul), 48

Christian Intelligencer and Mission Field (magazine), 56

Church Herald (magazine), 84

Church World Service, 46

Coakley, John W., *101, 104*

Collier, John W.P., 44, *45*

Collins, Charles G., 44

Condict, Ira, 5, *5*

Cone, James

Congregational churches, 62

Conover, Garret W., 30

Cook, George H., 32

Cornell, James A.H., 31–32, *33*, 104

Corwin, Edward T., xviii, 21, 32

De Hope (newspaper), 41

Demarest, David D., 8, 10, *12*, 45, 50

Demarest, Leah, 50

Demarest, William H.S., 24, 58–61, *59, 60*, 62, 64–65

Dennis, Warren, *9*, 102

Depression (of 1930s), 61, 65

De Velder, Walter, 70, *71*

De Vries, Thomas, *78*

De Witt, John, the elder, 14, *14*

De Witt, John, the younger, 39, 42–43, *42*, 100

Do, Enu Ju, 93

Doty, Clarissa, 20, *21*

Doty, Elihu, 20, *21*

Du Bois, Ray, *104*

Edinburgh Missionary Conference (1910), 45

Erasmus Hall, *4*

Erskine, Noel, 112 n.35

Index

Esmark, Eileen Winter, *95*
Evening Theological Education Program (ETEP), 86–89, *88*

faculty, approval of by students (1927), 59; constituting of, 12–13; duties of in Rutgers (Queen's) College, 24–25; inaugural lectures of, *4*, 64–65; and library, 39; in relation to superintendents, 12–13, 16–17
faculty residences, 30, *31*, 33, *34*, *35*, 67, *83*
field education (supervised ministry), 60, 91, 994, 102
Foreman, James, 90
French, Lawrence, 56
Fries, Paul, 78, *78*, *86*, 103
Froeligh, Solomon, 4
fundamentalism, 56

Gardner A. Sage Library. *See* Sage Library
Gates, Walter, 73
General Synod of the Reformed Church in America: Board of Direction of, 51; call of, for explanation from McClelland, 15; changes in relationship of, to seminary, 51, 55; changes to Board of Superintendents by, 35; changing relation of, to seminaries, 55, 60; covenants of, with Rutgers (Queen's) College, 5–6, 21–25; decision of, concerning Kansfield, 100; decision of, concerning Milledoler, 17–18; decision of, to form Classis of Amoy, 21; election of Demarest by, 58; election of professors, 1; election of Shedd by, 37; election of Worcester by, 62; establishment of office of professor, 2; establishment of theological instruction at Hope College by, 40–41; formation of Black Council by, 90; merger of seminary boards by, 76; Permanent Committee on Theological Education of, 73; prohibition by, of student preaching, 16–17; refusal of, to exclude Freemasons from church membership, 42; support by, of mission to Borneo, 21
General Synod professors, 100

German Reformed Church (Reformed Church in the United States), 15–16
Gillespie, John H., *52*, 57, *57*, *61*
Glover–Williams, Bernadette, *104*
Graves Lectures on mission, 49, 70
Graves, N.F., 49

Hackensack, Reformed Church of, 4
Hageman, Howard G., 32, 64, 72–73, 80, 84–88
Hartford Seminary, 62
Heidelberg Catechism, 63
Hertzog, Anna, 28
Hertzog Hall (The Peter Hertzog Theological Hall), *29*, 30, *31*, *35*, *56*; building of, 28–29; improvements of, 29–30, 36–37; demolition of, 73–75, *74*, 104
Hill, William Bancroft, 56
Hill-Alto, L'Anni, *94*
Hiram Street Project, 80–81
Hoffman, Milton, *60*, 65, *65*, 67
Hoffman, Robert, *78*
Hope College, 40
Hospers, Gerrit, 64
House, Renee, *101*, *104*
Hwang, Minkyung, *93*

Illinois College (Jacksonville, Illinois), 76
India, mission to. *See* Arcot Mission
International Missionary Council, 46
International Summer School of Theology (Netherlands), 103
Inter–Seminary Missionary Alliance, 49

Jamaica (Queens), NY, First Reformed Church in, 88
James, M. Stephen, 65, *66*, *68*
James, Marjorie, 67
Jamison, Wallace N., *66*, 73, 76, *76*

Janssen, Allan, 103
Jeon, Mill, *93*
Johnson, Edward P., *61*
Johnson, Elizabeth, 96, *96*, *101*
Johnson, William L., 112 n.35

Kansfield, Norman, 92–93, 98, *98*, 100
Kaufman, Gordon, 76
Kim, Eun–yul (Joel), *93*
Kim, Guncheol, and family *93*
Kim, Jinhong, *93*, 103, *104*
Kim, Wonhyo Titus, *93*
Koops, Hugh, 77, *101*
Kooy, Vernon, 33, 114 n.42
Korea, 46, *67*, 103
Korean Student Organization (KOSAN), *93*
Kuyper, Lester, 79

Lansing, John G., 38, 48, *48*, 49
Lee, Eung Wha, 67
Lee, Jiae, *93*
Lee, Youngmin, and family, *93*
Lim, Jin–Pyoung, and family, *93*
Livingston, John H., *1*, *10*, 107; as president and professor of Queen's College, 6; election of, as professor, 1; residence of, in New York, 3–4; residences of, in New Brunswick, 7–8, *8*; and slavery, 10
Ludlow, John, 13
Luidens, Edwin, 70

Mabon, William A., 46
Mack, Alma, *90*
MacLean, Hugh B., 68–69, 100
Marck, Johannes à, 17
Mast, Gregg, 98, *98*, 105
Master of Divinity degree, 77

McAndrews, Robert, *78*
McClelland, Alexander, 14–15, *15*, 24
McClendon, Rufus, 92
McMickle, Marvin, 91
Meeter, Daniel, *104*
Mercersburg theology, 15–16
Milledoler, Philip, 13, *13*; controversy over teaching of, 17–18; resignation from faculty, 18
Miller, Klaire, 94
Ministers' Conferences, annual, 59
Missionary House, 61, 70; moving of, 72, *72*
missions, foreign, 18–21, 45–49
modernism, 56, 64, 69
Modernization Fund, 67
Montgomery, NY, Reformed Church in, 37
Mook, Ruth, 67
Moros, Matilde, *104*
Mulder, True Wager, 95
Muste, Abraham J., 51, *51*, 66

National Black Economic Development Conference, 90
Neilson, James, 28
Neo–orthodoxy, 69
Nevin, John Williamson, 15
New Brunswick, NJ, city of, 6–11, *7*, *9*
New Brunswick Development Corporation (DEVCO), 103
New Brunswick Theological Seminary: 175th anniversary of, *66;* centennial of, 45; changing relationship of, with Reformed Church, 96–100; compared to plans of Princeton and Andover, 11–12; diversity as priority of, 91–95; fund-raising for, 30–33, 35–36, 51–52, 67, 71–73, 104; mission statements of, 96–98; name of, 40; plan of (1812); plan of (1923), 55–59; 11; sesquicentennial of, *63*; suspicions of, in Midwest, 43, 64, 69; *see also* campus; faculty
New Durham, New Jersey, Reformed Church in, 46

Index

New Jersey Board of Education, 60
New York, Central Reformed Church in, 37
New York, Collegiate Reformed Church in, 3, 23; Garden Street edifice, *4*
New York Theological Seminary, collaboration with, 87
Noe, Sydney, *40*

Old School Presbyterians, 15
Opiuim Wars, 20
Otterness, Richard, *78*

Paulsen, Bertha
Peale, Norman V., 66
Pohlmann, John, 20
Pohlmann, Theodosia, 20
Presbyterian Board of Foreign Missions, 47
Princeton Theological Seminary, 11–12, 27, 56, 59
professorships: first, 1; second, 13; third, 14; fourth, *14*; fifth, 37; sixth, 38, 51; of Metro-Urban Ministry, *91*
Progress Campaign, 53

Queen's College. *See* Rutgers College
Quick, Peter, 36, *36*

Rauschenbusch, Walter, 50
Raven, John H., *52*, 58, *61*, 105
Reformed Church Center, 99, *99*
Reformed Church in America: Articles of Union of, 2; Board of Foreign Missions of, 47–48; Board of Publication of, 60; boards and funds of, 53; confessional standards of, 58, 63–64, 69; Executive Committee of, 79; General Program Council of, 79; name changed from Reformed (Protestant) Dutch Church, 36; relation between eastern and midwestern regions, 40–43, 64, 68–69; *see also* General Synod of the Reformed Church in America

Reformed Church in the United States. *See* German Reformed Church
Reformed (Protestant) Dutch Church. *See* Reformed Church in America
Revivalism, 15
Richmond, Archie, *91*
Ridder, Herman, 76–79, *79*
Rogers, Virgil, *79*, *86*, 114 n.42
Romeyn, Dirck, 4
Rutgers College: building ("Old Queen's"),6–7, *7*, *8*; charter of, as Queen's College *4*, 5; closed and re-opened, 23; covenants of, with General Synod, 5–6, 21–25; interest of, in seminary campus, 73; named, 24; Neilson campus of, 34; sale of campus for use by, 103; theological professors' residences in, 8
Rutgers University. *See* Rutgers College

Saemoonan Presbyterian Church (Seoul), *47*
Sage, Gardner A., 32, *34*, 37, 104
Sage Library (The Gardner A. Sage Library), 33, *35*, 38–40, *38*, *40*, *41*, *83*, *92;* addition to, 61; renovation of, 104, *105*; Scholte Reading Court of, 105, *105*
St. John's University, 89, *89*
Schaff, Philip
Schenck, Ferdinand, 49–50, *52*
Schenectady, First Reformed Church in, 4
Schureman, John, 13
scripture, authority of, 68–69
Scudder Hall, 72, *74*, *75*, 104
Scudder, Harriet, 46
Scudder, Jared, 46, *46*, 111 n.43
Scudder, John, 46
Searle, John P., *52*, *61*
Seawood, James, 89, *90*, *101*
Seminary Sunday, 67
Shedd, William G.T., 37

Six Mile Run Reformed Church (Franklin, NJ), 14
Sizoo, Joseph R., 65, 67, *67*, 69
slavery, 10–11
Smith, Raynard, *104*
Social Christianity, 51
Social Gospel, 49–50
Society of Inquiry on Missions, 19, 32; allied with YMCA, 49
Somerville, NJ, United Reformed Church in, 103
spiritual disciplines, 102
Standing Committee on Hertzog Hall. See Standing Committee on Seminary Grounds and Property
Standing Committee on Seminary Grounds and Property, 36–38, 58
Steele, William H.
"Stone House," 32, *35*
Stout, Henry, *71*
student preaching, 16–17, 52–53, 60–61
students, residences of, 8
Sturm, Richard, *90*, 104
Sutton, Eugene, *101*
Suydam, James, 32, *33*, 37, 104
Suydam Hall, 32, *34*, *35*; demolition of, 73, 104
Talmage, John Van Nest, 21, *23*
Tanner, Beth, *104*
Taylor, Graham, 50, *50*
Tema, Eilia, 103, *103*
Thomas, Norman, 76, *79*, 80–81, *101*
Thomson, Frederick B., 20

Underwood, Horace G, 46–48, *47*, 103
Underwood Seminar, 103
Union Theological Seminary, 27, 37
United Synod Appeal (fund drive), 104

Vander Kolk, Eunice, 67

Vander Kolk, Justin, 71–73, *72*, 114 n.42
Van Dyke, John C., 40, *41*, 65
Van Vranken, Samuel, 13
Van Wyk, Julia, 67
Van Zandt, Abraham, 37
Virgil, Joseph De Cross, 44
Vosseller, Gladys, 67

Waanders, David, 78, *101*, *104*
Walden, Islay, 43–44, *43*
Warnshuis, Abbe L., 45–46, *45*
Washington, Wilbur, *70*, 91
Weber, William A., *60*, 65
Weis, Richard, *101*
Wesselink, Paul, *78*
Western Theological Seminary, 40, 55; proposals of merger of with, 73, 75; shared curriculum with, 76–80; shared ("unified") presidency with, 76–80
White, Robert, 86, 91, 97–98, *97*, 10, 103
Wilson, Margaret, 96
Winter, Egbert, 42–43, *43*
Wissink, Charles, *86*
women, in student body, 94–95, *95;* in faculty, 95–96
Woodbridge, Samuel, *47*, 52
Woodhull, Selah, 14
Worcester, Edward S., *60*, 62–65, *63*, 68–69, 100

YMCA (Young Men's Christian Association), 49, 56; in Korea, 48
Yonsei University, 48
Young, Archie, 44
Yu, Jay Do, *91*

Zwemer, Samuel, 48, *48*, 112 n.42
Zwemer Hall, *74*, 75, *83*